THE ROYAL AIR FORCE

The Memorabilia Collection

BY DAVID CURNOCK

This edition first published in the UK in 2006 by Green Umbrella Publishing

© Green Umbrella Publishing 2007

Printed and bound in China

ISBN: 978-1-905828-59-3

THE ROYAL AIR FORCE

The Memorabilia Collection

GreenUmbrella
Publishing

BY DAVID CURNOCK

THE ROYAL AIR FORCE *The Memorabilia Collection*

Contents

Chapter One	**Origins of the Royal Air Force**	6-21
Chapter Two	**The Trenchard Years and Beyond**	22-37
Chapter Three	**Early Overseas Operations**	38-45
Chapter Four	**Conflict on the Horizon**	46-63
Chapter Five	**Their Finest Hour**	64-83
Chapter Six	**A New Dawn**	84-101
Chapter Seven	**White Paper and White Bombers**	102-115
Chapter Eight	**The 60s and 70s**	116-133
Chapter Nine	**War and the Peace Dividend**	134-151
Chapter Ten	**Into the Future**	152-159

Chapter One

Origins of the Royal Air Force

RIGHT
British troops
crossing the Zand
River during the
Boer War campaign
in 1900. An
observation balloon
keeps watch for
enemy formations.

BELOW
Cartoon dated circa
1800. Proposed use
of balloons to raise
Highland Regiment
troops from where
they could fire at the
enemy as they
descended while
using their kilts as
parachutes.

Early Military Aviation

Throughout history, it has been shown that those who held the high ground gained a significant advantage over their adversaries in battle tactics. From a lofty vantage point the disposition of opposing armies could be observed, and their movements monitored, thus providing advance notice of any impending attack. The high ground also provided a useful platform for the firing of weapons, coupled with observation of their effect. However, the geography of theatres of war often failed to provide the convenient high ground that one combatant could use to gain advantage over the other. As time passed, man became more resourceful in overcoming the lack of elevated terrain features and at first used trees, later kites and balloons, to observe opposing forces.

Military aviation effectively began in Britain in 1878, with the formation by the Royal Engineers of a balloon unit. Their balloons were first used in the 1880s, during actions in the Sudan and in Bechuanaland, and later during the Boer War, in South Africa, between 1899 and 1902. The Royal Engineers also used man-carrying kites during the early 1900s. These were gradually superseded by powered airships, in 1907, and eventually by aeroplanes, with the formation of the first Royal Engineers Air Battalion in 1911. The development of the new British military air arm proceeded at a slow pace, there being only eleven qualified pilots by 1912, compared with over 260 pilots in the French Army Air Service at that time.

The Royal Flying Corps

The Royal Flying Corps (RFC) was constituted by Royal Warrant on April 13 1912, and took over the assets of the Royal Engineers Air Battalion on 13 May 1912. The RFC comprised a Military Wing, a Naval Wing, a Central Flying School (CFS) that was formed at Upavon, Wiltshire on June 19 1912, a Reserve force, and the Royal Aircraft Factory (formerly the Army Aircraft Factory) at Farnborough. The Military Wing was commanded by Captain

MAIN
Members of a Royal Flying Corps squadron on Salisbury Plain, Wiltshire, with a Royal Aircraft Factory B.E.2a aircraft, April 1913.

BELOW
RFC metal and cloth badges.

F.M.Sykes and comprised a Headquarters Unit, seven aeroplane squadrons, and one airship and man-carrying kite squadron.

The first recorded fatal aircraft accident involving an RFC aircraft occurred on July 5 1912, near to Stonehenge on Salisbury Plain,

Wiltshire, when the pilot, Captain Eustace B. Loraine, and his crewman observer, Staff-Sergeant R.H.V. Wilson, were killed. After this tragic event an order was issued, stating that "Flying will continue this evening as usual", thus beginning a tradition that has been maintained throughout the history of the RFC, and its successor, the Royal Air Force.

The B.E.2 biplane was adopted as the main fighter aircraft for the RFC and, by the end of 1912, there were three squadrons of B.E.2s with each squadron having 12 aircraft. A squadron of airships completed the inventory of powered flying machines. At the commencement of hostilities in 1914 the RFC used, in addition to the B.E.2, the Farman MF-7, the Avro 504, the Vickers FB5, the

Bristol Scout, and the F.E.2. By May 1915, the
RFC had a total of around 166 aircraft: that total
was a little over one-tenth of the aircraft inventory
of the French armed forces.

The first casualties of World War I sustained
by the RFC occurred in England on August 12
1914. Lieutenant Robert R. Skene and Air
Mechanic Ray Barlow lost their lives when their
aircraft crashed, en-route to a rendezvous with
others of the RFC, near Dover. Skene had
previously gained recognition for becoming the
first English pilot to perform a loop in an
aeroplane. Following the rendezvous, the RFC set
off for France in a mass crossing of the English
Channel with 60 machines.

The first action of the war undertaken by the
RFC was a two-aircraft reconnaissance mission on
August 19 1914. The operation was less than
successful due to the fact that, in order to save
weight, each aircraft carried only a pilot instead of
the usual crew of a pilot and an observer. Partly
due to this, and coupled with poor weather in the
area, both of the pilots lost their way and only one
was able to complete his task. The RFC achieved
its first victory on August 25 1914 when
Lieutenant C.W. Wilson and Lieutenant C.E.C.
Rabagliati took off in their Avro 504, and forced
down a German Etrich Taube observation aircraft
which had approached their aerodrome.

In April 1915, 2nd Lieutenant William
Barnard Rhodes-Moorhouse, No. 2 Squadron,
Royal Flying Corps became the first airman to be
awarded the Victoria Cross. After successfully
completing a bombing raid on the rail junction at
Kortrijk, Belgium, he received mortal wounds
from enemy fire but, in spite of his wounds,
brought his aircraft back to base and made his
report, before succumbing to his injuries the
following day.

In August 1915, the appointment of Major-
General Hugh Trenchard as RFC field

commander signalled the change to a more
aggressive approach to air warfare. Non-stop
patrols over enemy lines led to heavy casualties
and losses of aircraft. In July 1916, the RFC had a
total strength of 421 aircraft, equipping twenty-
seven squadrons, together with fourteen balloons
and four kite-balloon squadrons. At one point in
1916, two RFC aircrew were lost, on average,
every day and, by the springtime of 1917, aircraft
were being lost at the rate of almost fifty in a
week. Many of the losses were due to the superior
aircraft and equipment of the opposing forces at
that time. However, the lack of experience of
some of the RFC pilots coupled with the inherent
difficulty in controlling the effect of gyroscopic
forces, caused by the rotary engine on their
aircraft, was a contributing factor. The losses
diminished considerably after the arrival of newer,

improved fighter aircraft such as the Bristol Fighter, Sopwith Pup, Sopwith Camel, and S.E.5. As they gained experience with their new equipment, the RFC's fortunes improved to such an extent that it had gained superiority over the German Air Force before the end of 1917. With the advent of the Airco DH-4 high-altitude, single-engine bomber, and the Handley Page heavy bomber that was capable of striking industrial targets within Germany, Trenchard was able to carry out the strategic bombing for which he was a strong advocate.

One of the more unusual types of mission undertaken by the RFC was the delivery of intelligence agents behind enemy lines. The first such mission took place on the morning of September 13 1915, and ended in failure, as the aircraft crashed. The pilot, Captain T.W. Mulcahy-Morgan, and his passenger were both badly injured, and were captured. However, two years later, the pilot escaped, and returned to England. Later missions were more successful: in addition to delivering the agents, the RFC was also responsible for keeping them supplied with the carrier pigeons that were used to send their reports back to base. Eventually, in 1916, a Special Duty Flight was formed, as part of the Headquarters Wing, to handle these missions together with other unusual assignments.

On January 13 1917, an RFC officer, Captain Clive Collett made the first British military parachute jump from a heavier-than-air craft. The jump, from an altitude of some 600 feet, was successful but the hierarchy in the RFC, together with that of the Air Board, were opposed to the issuing of parachutes to aeroplane pilots. Their belief at the time was based on the premise that, in having a parachute, a pilot could be tempted into abandoning his aircraft in an emergency, rather than continue the fight, or bring it back to base. This policy remained in force until September 16 1918, when an order was issued for all single-seat aircraft to be fitted with parachutes.

Many of its pilots joined the RFC, from their original regiments, by first becoming an observer.

As no formal training was introduced for observers until 1917, many were sent on their first sortie with only a brief introduction to the aircraft from the pilot. Once certified as fully qualified, an observer was awarded the coveted half-wing 'O' brevet that, once awarded, could not be forfeited, so it essentially amounted to a decoration. Originally, the RFC observer was in command of the aircraft, while the pilot simply flew the machine. However, this was found to be less effective in combat than having the pilot in charge. Observers were usually given minimal flying training, sufficient only to be able to land their aircraft in case the pilot was killed or wounded. Experienced observers often volunteered, or were selected, for pilot training.

Eleven RFC members received the Victoria Cross during World War I. Initially, the RFC was against the publicising of both victory totals, and the exploits of their aircrews. However, due to immense interest from press and public, this policy was abandoned.

The Royal Naval Air Service

In the early 1900s, the Royal Navy used balloons and airships for aerial reconnaissance. In 1911, the Royal Navy's airship named Mayfly was destroyed before it flew, when its back was broken in strong winds. This event led to the naval minister of the time, Winston Churchill, to call for the development of military aircraft.

In December 1911, the Royal Naval Flying School was formed at Eastchurch, Kent. On the formation of the RFC in 1912, the Royal Navy was given the airships owned by the British Army. It was also given twelve aircraft, to be used in naval operations. The first flight from a moving ship took place in May 1912. A year later, the first seaplane carrier, named Hermes, was commissioned. Around this time, the Royal Navy began to build a series of coastal air stations in support of its aviation operations.

The Royal Naval Air Service (RNAS) was formally established in January 1914 and, soon after, had a total of 217 pilots and 95 aircraft, of

BELOW
Bristol Scout, 1916.

BELOW
No 1 Squadron pictured at Claremarais, France. Originally formed in 1878 as No. 1 Balloon Company, Royal Engineers, this squadron has been in continuous operation ever since 1912. Note the mascot beagle hound held by pilot (fourth from right).

which 55 were seaplanes or flying boats. These included the Curtiss H-16 flying boat, produced by Glenn Hammond Curtiss in the United States, that was one of the most successful aircraft of its type, reflected in the purchase of 64 for use by the RNAS in the reconnaissance and bomber roles. By the outbreak of the First World War, in August 1914, the RNAS had more aircraft under its control than did the RFC.

The main roles of the RNAS were fleet reconnaissance, patrolling coasts for enemy ships and submarines, attacking enemy coastal territory, and defending Britain from enemy air raids. The RNAS also operated fighter squadrons, equipped with the Bristol Scout, Sopwith Pup and Sopwith Camel, on the Western Front. The leading air ace of the RNAS was the Canadian-born Raymond Collishaw, with a total of 60 aircraft shot down, six of these in one day, and a further eight observation balloons destroyed.

The RNAS had been severely criticised for its failure in preventing the Zeppelin bombing raids on mainland Britain. In February 1916, there was

a change of policy, and the RFC was given the responsibility for dealing with Zeppelins once they were over Britain. The RNAS then turned its efforts to the bombing of Zeppelins at their bases in Germany.

By the early part of 1918, the RNAS was able to muster over 67,000 personnel, an inventory of almost 3,000 aircraft and more than one hundred airships, and 26 coastal stations. When absorbed into the new Royal Air Force, the RNAS squadrons were either renumbered, by the addition of 200 to their existing number, as in the case of No. 8 Squadron of the RNAS becoming No. 208 Squadron, Royal Air Force. Where units of the RNAS were previously without a squadron number, then these were allocated a squadron number in that '200' series.

The Royal Air Force –
A New Service is Created

As the war progressed, it became apparent to the Government that Britain's existing air arms had become unwieldy and inefficient due, in part, to inter-service rivalry, and also the lack of a

unified command structure. Problems in the supply of machines and equipment were apparent, creating shortages in some areas, as well as duplication in others. Either situation was both inefficient, and not for the common good.

In July 1917, the Prime Minister, David Lloyd George, appointed General Jan Smuts to report on the reasons for the equipment supply problems, and the effectiveness of the air defence of the country. The comprehensive Smuts report recommended the amalgamation of the two air arms, the RFC and RNAS, into a single organisation and command structure, and the creation of a new government ministry, with equal standing to the War Office and the Admiralty, to head the new air arm. The Air Forces (Constitution) Act, of November 29 1917, legislated for the establishment of an Air Ministry, similar to the Army Council and the Board of the Admiralty. The new ministry was tasked to plan for, and oversee, the amalgamation of the RFC and RNAS into one new body.

At first, the decision to create a new service was opposed by many, including Sir Hugh Trenchard himself, who believed that the prime purpose of the RFC was to support the Army in its operations and, similarly, the RNAS should do likewise for the Navy. He felt that the new service would not provide the same level of support to those services, together with his concerns about the long-term effects of combat fatigue on the pilots and aircrews. Under the RFC, pilots and observers were seconded from their regiments, and could return there when they were unable to continue with their flying duties. This arrangement would not be available in the new amalgamated body. However, Trenchard later changed his view, and was soon to accept the challenge of bringing the new body into being.

The new Air Council, under Major-General Sir Hugh Trenchard, came into being on January 3 1918, and was tasked with the structural organisation of the new service. Its remit included the provision for the transfer of personnel, the creation of rank and command structures, and also the disciplinary arrangements for the new service. Around this time there were many political differences, and personality clashes, between various members of the Council but, eventually, the new service took its place as the junior member of the British armed forces.

On April 1 1918, the Royal Air Force (RAF) became the world's largest, and the first truly independent, air force. Initially, the rank structure was the same as that of the British Army. Major-General Sir Hugh Trenchard, the Chief of Staff (CAS) was tasked with responsibility for the operational aspects of the RAF. His Deputy Chief of Staff (DCAS) was Major-General (formerly Rear-Admiral) Mark Kerr. Another two senior officers, namely, Major-General (formerly Commodore) Sir Godfrey Paine (Master-General of Personnel), and Major-General Edward

Ellington (Controller-General of Equipment), headed the main departments of the Air Staff. However, a combination of political differences and personal disagreements led to the resignation of Trenchard, who was replaced as CAS by Major-General Sir Frederick Sykes, on April 18 1918. Also formed that year was a female branch of the new air force, the Women's Royal Air Force, as was the Royal Air Force Nursing Service.

At the time of the Armistice, the Royal Air Force remained the largest air force in the world, with an inventory of 22,647 aircraft of all types, including 3,300 on its first-line strength, and 103 airships. These aircraft were operated by a total of 133 squadrons and 15 flights overseas, and another 55 squadrons in Britain. A further 75 squadrons were engaged in training. Royal Air Force units operated from a total of 401 aerodromes at home, and a further 274 overseas, with personnel totalling 27,333 officers and 263,837 other ranks.

The Royal Air Force Badge

The badge for the Royal Air Force was adopted at a meeting of the Air Council on August 1 1918. It has been claimed that a tailor at Gieves Ltd, the military tailors, had designed the badge. Furthermore, it is believed that he originally drew an albatross, not an eagle.

The design was similar to that of the current badge with the exception that the circlet surrounding the eagle was originally a garter and buckle. This design was never submitted for

Chapter One

approval. After an Air Council meeting in December 1922, the badge design was formalised and submitted to the College of Arms for registration a month later, after having been approved by the King, together with the design for a uniform. Several attempts to modify the badge have been resisted since the College of Arms drew the version with an eagle and a laurel surround. An authority on the subject – A New Dictionary of Heraldry – edited by Stephen Friar, and published in 1987, states that the official badge of the Royal Air Force has existed since 1949, with the heraldic description: *"In front of a circle inscribed with the motto Per Ardua Ad Astra and ensigned by the Imperial Crown an eagle volant and affronty Head lowered and to the sinister."*

"Per Ardua ad Astra"

The origin of the motto of the Royal Air Force is believed to date back to the formation of the Royal Flying Corps in 1912. The commander of the RFC Military Wing, now Colonel Frederick Sykes, later to become the CAS in 1918, tasked his officers to devise a motto for the new service that would both inspire and encourage a strong 'esprit de corps'. Anecdotally, two junior officers were discussing the subject of the motto and one of them, Lieutenant J.S.Yule, mentioned a phrase from Virgilian text: "Sicitar ad Astra". This, he developed into "Per Ardua ad Astra" which he translated as: "Through Struggles to the Stars". It is claimed that Yule had read the book called 'The People of the Mist', by Sir Henry Rider Haggard, in which the following passage appears in Chapter 1: *"To his right were two stately gates of iron fantastically wrought, supported by stone pillars on whose summit stood griffins of black marble embracing coats of arms and banners inscribed with the device Per Ardua ad Astra".* Colonel Sykes gave his formal approval, and submitted it to the War Office. The King then approved its adoption for use in the RFC.

The Royal Air Force Ensign

The introduction of the Royal Air Force Ensign, in 1920, was not a straightforward event, as it involved all three services. The Air Council had decided that the Royal Air Force should fly its own flag from its stations whereupon the Board of the Admiralty, who have the right to veto the introduction of any new flag to be used either on land or at sea within British territories, strongly objected to the idea. The Air Council remained adamant and, eventually, the Admiralty conceded, but with the proviso that the Royal Air Force should adopt a flag bearing the Union Flag, and with some other appropriate device thereon. Initially, the Air Council submitted a design that was, effectively, a White Ensign without the Cross of St. George: this was rejected by the Admiralty on the grounds that the White, Red, and Blue Ensigns were to be used exclusively by Naval services.

Many designs were considered, including some submitted by the general public. One idea put

LEFT
The Royal Air Force Badge. (© Crown Copyright)

RIGHT
The White Ensign design that was rejected by the Admiralty.

BELOW
The Royal Air Force Ensign.

forward was that the ensign should include the roundel of concentric red, white and blue circles, as this device had been used on aircraft of both the RFC and RNAS, and would be appropriate for use by the new service. A suggestion by Air Vice-Marshal Salmond that the Union Flag be incorporated in the top left-hand corner would show the mark of British authority. This design was accepted by the Admiralty, approved by His Majesty King George V, and introduced into service in December 1920. The new ensign was later protected by an Order in Council, signed by the King on March 24 1921, that protects both the status of the Royal Air Force Ensign, and its authorised use.

Use of the Royal Air Force Ensign

The Royal Air Force Ensign is flown daily at established RAF stations. The flag is formally raised by duty personnel just before commencement of daily duties, and lowered at the end of the working day: it is also raised and lowered on specific occasions such as unit parades.

At headquarters of major commands, and on ministry buildings, the flag is usually flown at the head of a staff on the top of the building. On

special occasions, and also on very large buildings for prominence and aesthetics, a flag having dimensions twice the normal size, of three feet by six feet, may be flown. On stations, the flag is flown from a flag staff in the pendant 'maritime' manner.

The Royal Air Force Ensign is not permitted to be displayed other than properly mounted on a mast or staff, and is never carried on a parade; nor may it be used as bunting, or for any other purpose. It is not correct to use the flag as a coffin drape at a funeral; it is proper to use the Union Flag for that purpose. In certain circumstances, the Royal Air Force Ensign is flown in place of the Union Flag, as demonstrated at the 'Border Posts' of the Sovereign Base Areas in Cyprus.

BELOW
The Royal Air Force flag being lowered at Station Headquarters RAF Gan for the last time after the airfield was handed over to the Republic of Maldives in 1976.

RIGHT
The Royal Air
Force Roundel.

BELOW
RAF aeroplanes
making their
presence felt in
Egypt with the
roundal clearly
visible, 1925.

The Royal Air Force Roundel

During World War I, it became apparent that there was a need to identify aircraft in order to avoid confusion between enemy and friendly forces. In August 1914, orders were given for the Union Flag to be painted on the underside of the lower wings of all front line aircraft. Although this marking appeared satisfactory at lower levels, at altitude only the cross was clearly visible, and was often mistaken for the German cross. It was then decided to adopt the French style of concentric circles, but with the red and blue rings transposed. A smaller version of the Union Flag was retained

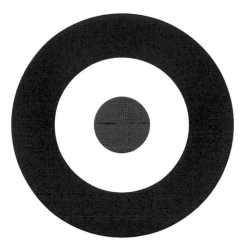

between the roundels and the wingtips, and a miniature Union Flag was painted on the rudder. Aircraft of the Naval Wing of the RFC were marked with one red ring and the Union Flag.

In May 1915, the Union Flag on the aircraft rudder was replaced by red, white and blue vertical stripes and, in June of that year, the roundel was additionally painted on the upper surface of the wings. These roundels and stripes formed the basis for RAF aircraft identifying markings for many years into the future. The roundel has evolved, along with the various aircraft camouflage and colour scheme changes through the years, in order to reflect the differing aircraft roles and/or their theatres of operations.

Royal Air Force Medals

Before the formation of the Royal Air Force its personnel were either members of the RFC, that was part of the Army, or the RNAS, part of the Royal Navy. As members of those services, they were eligible for their respective service's medals and awards. It was also possible for personnel from one service to be awarded medals from another branch of the armed forces, for acts performed while on duty with that service. For example, a member of the Army could be awarded a Royal Navy decoration for service on board a RN vessel.

On June 3 1918, four new medals were instituted that could be awarded for acts of exceptional gallantry in the air: a Bar could be added to any of the four medals, in recognition of any subsequent award. The four new medals were the Distinguished Flying Cross (DFC), Distinguished Flying Medal (DFM), Air Force Cross (AFC), and Air Force Medal (AFM). The DFC and DFM were to be awarded for acts of bravery during active service flying operations, and the AFC and AFM for bravery during non-operational flying. The crosses (DFC and AFC)

Distinguished Flying Cross   Air Force Cross

Distinguished Flying Medal   Air Force Medal

**ROYAL AIR FORCE MEDALS
FOR GALLANTRY IN THE AIR**

were awarded to commissioned officers and warrant officers, and the medals (DFM and AFM) were the equivalent awards for other ranks.

The DFM and AFM were discontinued as a result of the 1993 review. Since that year, the DFC and AFC have both been made available for award to all ranks.

RIGHT
Sir Hugh Trenchard,
1st Viscount,
Marshal of the RAF,
in his uniform,
displaying several
of his medals.

Chapter Two

The Trenchard Years and Beyond

LEFT
Sir Hugh Trenchard.

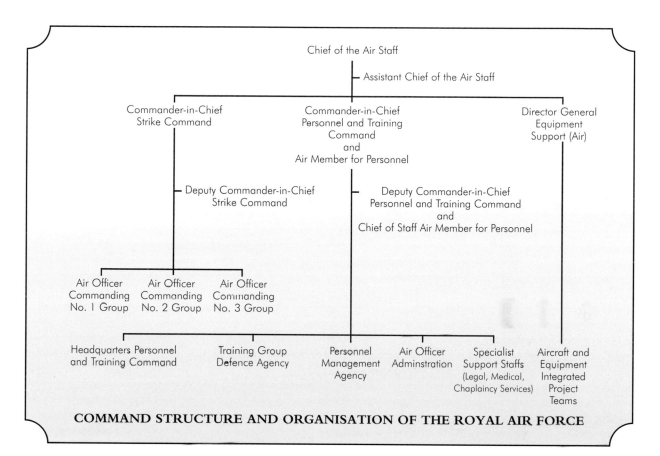

Chief of the Air Staff

Assistant Chief of the Air Staff

Commander-in-Chief
Strike Command

Commander-in-Chief
Personnel and Training
Command
and
Air Member for Personnel

Director General
Equipment
Support (Air)

Deputy Commander-in-Chief
Strike Command

Deputy Commander-in-Chief
Personnel and Training Command
and
Chief of Staff Air Member for Personnel

Air Officer
Commanding
No. 1 Group

Air Officer
Commanding
No. 2 Group

Air Officer
Commanding
No. 3 Group

Headquarters Personnel
and Training Command

Training Group
Defence Agency

Personnel
Management
Agency

Air Officer
Adminstration

Specialist
Support Staffs
(Legal, Medical,
Chaplaincy Services)

Aircraft and
Equipment
Integrated
Project
Teams

COMMAND STRUCTURE AND ORGANISATION OF THE ROYAL AIR FORCE

Two of the most significant events in the history of the Royal Air Force occurred in 1919: the first being the appointment of Winston Churchill as Secretary of State for War and Air on January 11 1919. The second was the return of Sir Hugh Trenchard as Chief of the Air Staff in February of that year, a position held until his retirement in 1929. The appointment of Trenchard was a milestone in the history of the Royal Air Force, as it was he who led the fledgling service from the dark days of war into the light of a bright new future. The RAF was shaped under his command and guidance, and his efforts in that regard earned him the affectionate, albeit unofficial, title of 'Father of the RAF'.

Trenchard, by then an Air Marshal, was responsible for drafting the White Paper that was introduced into Parliament, by Churchill, in 1919 that outlined the proposed structure, organisation and development of the Royal Air Force in the years following the end of World War I. The White Paper is commonly known as the Trenchard Memorandum.

Its contents laid down the requirement for disposition of squadrons, both at home and overseas, as well as providing the structure for the personnel training establishments for the service. These included the Royal Air Force College, Staff College, and the Apprentice School.

Royal Air Force Command Structure

The command structure of the Royal Air Force has remained almost unchanged since its conception in 1919, although the functions and titles of some of the elements have changed to reflect the different requirements of the service since that year. Political control over the RAF was delegated by Parliament to the Air Ministry until 1964, when it passed to the Ministry of Defence. Up to 1964, the Air Council was the overall controlling body and was composed of service officers and politicians. With the

Commands have been formed either on a functional, or geographic, basis as dictated by prevailing military or political requirements through the years. Since 1919, there has been a total of 48 separate commands created at home including Bomber, Fighter, Coastal, Transport, Signals, Balloon, Maintenance, Flying Training, and Technical Training. Overseas commands date from 1918, when the first to be created in Europe were those carried

abolition of the Air Ministry in 1964, Senior Air Officer staff members remained within the new Defence Council, as heads of their respective Air Staff Departments, with responsibility for policy-making and procurement under direct control of the Chief of Air Staff (CAS).

Commands

Within the Royal Air Force, operational control is delegated to 'Commands', each usually under the control of an Air Officer Commanding–in–Chief (AOC-in-C). The various

over from the RFC that became, respectively, the HQ Royal Air Force, under Major-General Sir John Salmond, and the Independent Force, under Major-General Sir Hugh Trenchard. Since the period of the early 1920s, a total of 11 commands were created in Europe, 56 in the Middle East, and 36 in total throughout Iraq, India, South East Asia and the Far East.

Many new commands were formed during the period covering the 1939-45 war, both at home and overseas. In the latter part of the 1960s, it was decided that the reduction in size of the Royal Air

MAIN
Trainee Royal Air Force pilots in flight in Avro Anson machines in 1940. The Anson entered the war with Coastal Command squadrons engaged in reconnaissance and convoy escort duties.

Force did not warrant such a large command structure. As a result, in 1968, Bomber and Fighter Commands were combined to form the new Strike Command. Subsequently, on November 28 1969, they were joined by the former Coastal Command that was renamed to become No. 18 (Maritime Group). On September 1 1972, Air Support Command (formerly Transport Command) was integrated into Strike Command to form two new groups, No. 38 Group (Tactical Support), and No. 46 Group (Strategic Support). In the new command structure, the former Maintenance and Training Commands were amalgamated under the new RAF Support Command. This new command was itself subsequently divided into Personnel and Training Command, and Logistics Command on April 1 1994. In due course, Logistics Command was disbanded on April 1 2000, when it was integrated into the new Defence Logistics Organisation.

Strike Command is the larger of the two commands and bears responsibility for all aircraft operations, wherever they may be required, at home and overseas. Within Strike Command, three groups control different aspects of aircraft operations. No. 1 Group is known as the Air Combat Group, and operates all fast jet combat aircraft. No. 2 Group, otherwise known as the Air Combat Support Group, operates logistic support transport aircraft, both fixed and rotary wing, and air-to-air refuelling tankers. No. 3 Group, is the Air Battle Management Group, and controls the maritime patrol and reconnaissance aircraft, and the Search and Rescue (SAR) helicopters from their UK coastal bases, as well as the Mountain Rescue Service. Additionally, No. 3 Group controls all Airborne Early Warning (AEW) aircraft and ground based air defence radar installations throughout the UK. In its guise as Battle Management control, No. 3 Group has

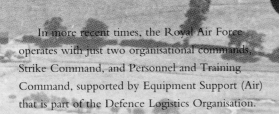

In more recent times, the Royal Air Force operates with just two organisational commands, Strike Command, and Personnel and Training Command, supported by Equipment Support (Air) that is part of the Defence Logistics Organisation.

command of all assets for homeland defence and overseas deployment operations, including Intelligence and the Surveillance, Target Acquisition and Reconnaissance (STAR) functions.

Personnel and Training Command controls all aspects of personnel management from recruiting, training, career management and development, welfare and conditions of service for all regular, reserve, or civilian personnel serving within the Royal Air Force. Sub-divisions are responsible for specialist areas of management, including Agencies for Personnel Management, Training, Administration, and support staffs for Royal Air Force Legal, Medical, and Chaplaincy Services. The Headquarters Unit also controls Air Cadets, University Air Squadrons, and the Royal Air Force Aerobatic Team, The Red Arrows.

Groups, Stations and Squadrons

Within the individual commands, lower levels of operational control are delegated to 'Groups', each usually commanded by an Air Officer Commanding (AOC). A Group performs specific operational roles within the main functional role of the overall Command, according to its location or other service requirement. Establishments such as the Royal Air Force College report directly to the Ministry of Defence, and usually have 'Group' status, with their commanding officer given the title of Commandant.

Groups can control a number of 'Stations', each Station being headed by a station commander designated as Officer Commanding. A station can have a number of sub-ordinate units based on it, these units either reporting directly to their controlling Group, or to the 'host' station commander. Prior to World War II, RAF stations usually hosted a single 'Squadron' or unit and the head of the squadron or unit was, in most cases, also the station commander. Hostilities led to an increase in the number of units based at some stations. During the war, several stations were grouped together under the command of a Base Commander, usually with the rank of Air Commodore.

'Wings' are either sub-divisions of stations, or can be an independent part of a group. Traditionally, a wing was a number of squadrons, combining for operational purposes. Today's stations usually have three wings; Operations, Engineering, and Administrative: each of these wings may comprise a number of 'squadrons'.

A squadron is the title for a unit that, in the operational flying role, is comparable to an army regiment in that it can have traditions and a history, regardless of its present role or operational status, and can be awarded standards and battle honours. These awards and traditions are retained under the squadron number, even in instances where the squadron's role is changed from that for which the honours were awarded, or until it is disbanded. Whenever such a squadron is reformed, it is entitled to display its predecessor squadron's battle honours and awards.

Non-flying squadrons form a sub-division of a wing, based on the function performed, and do not have the 'regimental' style of traditions or awards. Squadrons are themselves sub-divided into 'Flights', and these flights may also be sub-divided into 'Sections', according to their functional roles.

Equipment Support (Air)

Equipment Support (Air) is responsible for engineering and supply support for all Royal Air Force, Royal Navy, and Army aircraft, and operates as a number of Integrated Project Teams (IPT), each being responsible for one particular type of aircraft or equipment. An IPT is funded to provide the necessary equipment support for the aircraft or equipment type within its area of responsibility.

Branch Structure

Before the formation of the Royal Air Force in 1918, officers in both the RFC and RNAS were seconded from their regiments or naval units.

RIGHT
A group of fighter pilots from No. 32 Squadron relaxing at the RAF Fighter Squadron HQ at Hawkinge, Kent in 1940.

1940

General Duties, General Duties (Air Gunners) General Duties (Air Observer), Technical (Engineers), Technical (Signals) Technical (Armament), Balloon, ASD (for Administrative duties), ASD (for Intelligence duties), ASD (for Marine Craft duties), ASD (for Photographic duties), ASD (for PT duties), ASD (for Assistant Provost Marshal duties), ASD (for Special duties) Meteorological, Equipment, Accountant Medical, Dental, Chaplain, Legal

1945

General Duties, General Duties (Air Gunners), Wireless Operator (Air), General Duties (Flight Engineers), General Duties (Navigators), General Duties (Navigaton Instructors), General Duties (Meteorological Observers), Technical (Engineers), Technical (Electrical Engineers), Technical (Signals), Technical (Armament), Technical (Airfield Construction), Balloon ASD (for Administrative duties and Miscellaneous duties), ASD (Special Duties (Armament)), ASD (Special Duties (Engineers)), ASD (Special Duties (Marine Craft)), ASD (Special Duties (MT)), ASD (Special Duties (Photography)), ASD (Special Duties (Signals)), Equipment, Accountant, Medical, Dental, Chaplain, Legal, Meteorological, RAF Regiment

1980

General Duties, General Duties (Ground) Photographic Interpretation, Engineer, Supply, Administrative, Security, Marine, Medical, Dental, Princess Mary's RAF Nursing Service, Medical Technician (Medical Section), Medical Technician (Dental Section), Medical Secretarial, Chaplains, Legal, Directors of Music

1996

General Duties, General Duties (Ground) (Air Traffic Control), General Duties (Ground) (Fighter Control), General Duties (Ground) (Intelligence), Engineer, Supply, Administrative (Secretarial), Administrative (Training), Administrative (Catering), Administrative (Physical Education), Security (RAF Regiment), Security (Provost), Medical, Dental, Princess Mary's RAF Nursing Service, Medical Technician (Medical Section), Medical Technician (Dental Section), Medical Secretarial, Chaplains, Legal, Directors of Music

BRANCH STRUCTURE

Their promotion prospects were limited to those afforded strictly according to seniority and establishment vacancy within their original units. Without a particular specialisation, an officer's prospects for advancement were very poor. One way of achieving a more rapid promotion was for an officer to transfer to another unit, or to become a Staff Officer, and then be eligible for promotion on the Army List. A broadly similar system also applied to officers of the RNAS. The Army List gazetted these officers under the appointment held within their respective organisation, for example,

as Staff Officer, Wing, Squadron or Flight Commander, or simply Flying Officer.

On the formation of the Royal Air Force, a Branch structure was created wherein all officers were placed in a specific Branch of the service according to the role they fulfilled. Officers were transferred between the various Branches depending upon the particular post held, or to be filled. This system also allowed for those officers qualified as pilots to carry out Staff Officer or other administrative duties: in this way, their promotion prospects could be enhanced. Furthermore, there was also some provision for retaining officers within the service if they became either unfit, or were no longer required, for flying duties.

Originally, there were eight officer Branches created:

(1) Aeroplane and Seaplanes – for qualified pilots employed on flying duties.

(2) Administrative – for officers employed on Administration duties (even if qualified as pilots).

(3) Airship – for officers qualified and employed on flying duties on Airships.

(4) Kite Balloon – for officers employed to man the Kite Balloon sections.

(5) Medical – for Medical Officers (previously provided by the RAMC, for the RFC, and the RN, for the RNAS).

(6) Observer – for officers qualified and employed on observer duties in aeroplanes

(7) Staff Officer – for those officers employed on staff duties at Headquarters units.

(8) Technical – for officers employed on Maintenance, Supply and similar duties.

Trenchard himself took the decision that, except for a very few particularly specialised branches, all of his officers should be pilots. The exceptions were the Medical, Accountant, and Equipment Branches. All other officers would be qualified as pilots and placed in the General Duties (GD) Branch, where they would be responsible for all functional aspects of the Royal Air Force including flying, supervision of engineering, and carrying out staff and administrative duties. The GD Branch also provided the commanders of all operational units: officers within the Branch were eligible for promotion to the highest ranks of the new rank structure. However, officers in the three specialised branches could only aspire to command units within their Branch of specialisation, with their prospective promotion ceiling being that of the highest rank allocated to their particular

branch. This new, and smaller, branch structure remained virtually unchanged until the 1930s when, due to a large increase in the requirement for officers resulting from the build-up of the service prior to World War II, many new units were formed. Many of these units had no requirement for a qualified pilot, and some of the new stations required autonomous headquarters staffs that were independent of the resident squadrons and units.

At the beginning of the war, specialists were being engaged on a 'for the duration of hostilities only' basis, often in posts that did not fit into the existing branch structure. Prior to 1940, officers in the specialist engineering, armament and signals functions had first been trained as pilots then, after a period on squadron duties, had completed their training on a course of instruction at the relevant specialist training school. Having been trained in their specialisation, they would then alternate these duties with those normally associated with a General Duties Officer, either in a flying post, or as a staff officer. However, the growing complexity of modern aircraft and equipment was beginning to demand a greater degree of specialisation than could be provided by such 'temporary' technical staff. As a result, it was decided to form a separate Technical Branch, with the sub-divisions of Engineering, Signals and Armament.

Officers that were sufficiently qualified were transferred to this new branch, although for many years, officers would still be moved between the GD and Technical branches, as they alternated between operational flying and technical postings. The GD Branch was also the subject of further change from 1939, when the decision was taken to designate Air Gunners as official members of aircrew. Until then, air gunners had been recruited from the ground staff, and given extra pay for undertaking these duties: on cessation of flying duties, they reverted to their ground trades. The majority of air gunners were appointed to the rank of sergeant, but some were commissioned, to act as gunnery leaders. By the end of WW2, some air gunners had actually risen to command squadrons. Another addition to the GD Branch occurred with the inclusion of Air Observers, who were needed in the new multiple-crew aircraft to relieve the pilots of the additional tasks of navigation and bomb aiming.

The increased administrative demands of the enlarged wartime RAF were satisfied by the recruitment and appointment of retired officers, academics, and qualified administrators, who were commissioned into another new branch, named Administrative and Special Duties Branch (ASD), again with a number of specialised sub-divisions. The Branch Structure underwent four major revisions, first in 1940, then in 1945, 1980 and 1986.

On April 1 1997, the Operations Support branch was formed. This new branch comprised four of the existing sub-branch specialisations, Operations Support (Air Traffic Control), Operations Support (Fighter Control), Operations Support (Intelligence) and Operations Support (RAF Regiment), and added a new branch of Operations Support (Flight Operations).

The Flight Operations sub-branch was created to utilise specially trained officers in operations posts, as well as in headquarters posts that had previously been filled by aircrew officers on ground tours. Most of the Flight Operations officers would be ex-aircrew, thereby removing them from the General Duties list, and thus freeing posts at the higher levels. This would have an additional benefit in that it would provide opportunities for advancement, for junior officers that were not previously available. A less popular feature of this situation was that officers in the new sub-branch would be able to utilise their

experience in flight operational matters but without the benefit of receiving flying pay.

ROYAL FLYING CORPS OFFICER RANKS INSIGNIA

Ranks and Badges of the Royal Air Force

In the period prior to August 27 1919, the Royal Air Force used rank titles of the British Army. From that date, a new rank structure was introduced, based on rank titles from both the Army and the Royal Navy, together with some newly created designations.

Commissioned ranks within the Royal Navy were used as the basis for the ranks of Air Commodore, Group Captain, Wing Commander,

RFC NON-COMMISSIONED RANKS BADGES

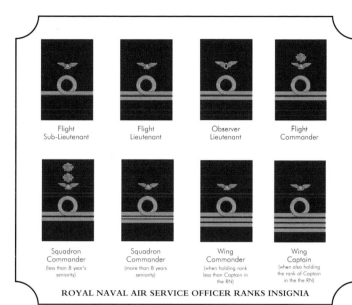

Flight Sub-Lieutenant | Flight Lieutenant | Observer Lieutenant | Flight Commander

Squadron Commander (less than 8 year's seniority) | Squadron Commander (more than 8 years seniority) | Wing Commander (when holding rank less than Captain in the RN) | Wing Captain (when also holding the rank of Captain in the the RN)

ROYAL NAVAL AIR SERVICE OFFICER RANKS INSIGNIA

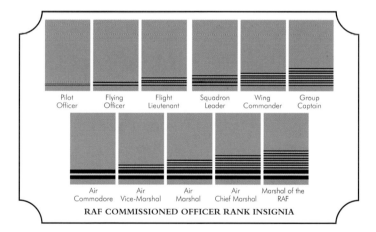

Pilot Officer | Flying Officer | Flight Lieutenant | Squadron Leader | Wing Commander | Group Captain

Air Commodore | Air Vice-Marshal | Air Marshal | Air Chief Marshal | Marshal of the RAF

RAF COMMISSIONED OFFICER RANK INSIGNIA

Leading Aircraftsman | Senior Aircraftsman | Junior Technician | Corporal | Sergeant | Chief Technician

Flight Sergeant | Warrant Officer | Sergeant Aircrew | Flight Sergeant Aircrew | Master Aircrew

RANK BADGES FOR NCOs, NON-COMMISSIONED AIRCREW AND OTHER RANKS

Squadron Leader, and Flight Lieutenant. New ranks of Flying Officer and Pilot Officer were introduced at the lower end of the ladder. The more senior ranks, of Air Vice-Marshal and above, were also based on those of either navy or army origin. The commissioned rank structure in the RAF has remained, virtually unchanged, since 1919.

The non-commissioned officer (NCO) ranks, also created in 1919, were broadly those of the Army, except for the new rank of Flight Sergeant which took precedence over that of Sergeant. In the years that followed there were several changes in the rank structure for NCOs: in April 1933, the rank of Sergeant Major was abolished, leaving Warrant Officer Class 1 and Class 2 at the top of the ladder. Later, during World War II, the Warrant Officer 2 rank was abolished, thus leaving 'Warrant Officer,' without numerical designator, as the senior non-commissioned rank.

Rank title changes for NCOs and other ranks have taken place at various times throughout the life of the RAF. Some new ranks were created for the new 'technician' rank structure that was introduced during the 1950s. In this structure, specific rank titles were given to personnel who had a technical or other specialisation, including aircraft engineering, and ground engineering tradesmen, bandsmen, and others. The technician rank held, and the subsequent promotion to higher level, was by attainment of qualifications gained after examinations of technical knowledge and ability, general service training (including knowledge of service administration and organisation), and with a minimum time limitation in a rank before advancement to a higher level. In exceptional circumstances, according to service requirements, the time limitation was reduced, or sometimes waived, and the promotion was deemed 'accelerated'. Technicians were also eligible for promotion to the next-highest rank on the normal 'command' promotion ladder, a situation that was not popular with 'non-technician' ranks who were awaiting elevation to the higher echelons.

The new technician ranks that were introduced in 1951 ranged from Junior Technician (no previous rank equivalent), Corporal Technician (equivalent to Corporal), Senior Technician (equivalent to Sergeant), Chief Technician (equivalent to Flight Sergeant), and Master Technician (equivalent to Warrant Officer). The Junior Technician insignia was an inverted single chevron; those for Corporal, Senior, and Chief Technicians were inverted versions of their equivalent 'command ' rank's chevrons. In the 1960s, the inverted chevrons were abolished, the four-bladed propeller insignia replacing both the single 'stripe' of the Junior Technician, and the crown of the Chief Technician that had surmounted the three inverted 'stripes' that were now positioned point-downward.

Only two technician rank titles exist in the modern day RAF, those of Junior Technician and Chief Technician; the remaining technician levels are covered within the normal ranking structure. Since 1950, non-commissioned aircrew members are awarded NCO rank badges and titles similar to those of the standard NCO rank structure surmounted by a brass spread-eagle. However, the rank equivalent to Warrant Officer is that of 'Master Aircrew'. Those holding this rank are given the title that indicates their specialisation, i.e. Master Signaller (MSig), Master Engineer (MEng), Master Air Electronics Operator (MAEOp) and Master Air Loadmaster (MALM).

Colleges and Training Schools

The Royal Air Force College at Cranwell in Lincolnshire is the oldest Air Force College in the world. The college was originally a naval training school for flying training and airship operations and was commissioned as 'The Royal Naval Air Service Central Training Establishment Cranwell' on April 1 1916, under the command of Commodore Godfrey M, Paine. A Boys' Training Wing was also established at Cranwell to train naval ratings as riggers and air mechanics. After the amalgamation of the RFC and RNAS on April 1 1918, the base was transferred under the control of the new Royal Air Force and renamed Royal Air Force Station Cranwell.

The Chief of Air Staff, Sir Hugh Trenchard was convinced of the requirement for trained officers to lead the new service into the future, and from these officers would become the future commanders of the service. One of his first actions on taking command was to establish a college that would provide the military and flying training for his officer cadets. In a biography it is quoted that the reason Trenchard chose Cranwell as the location in which his cadets should undergo their training was because: *"Marooned in the wilderness, cut off from pastimes they could not organise for themselves, the cadets would find life cheaper, healthier and more wholesome."*

Originally formed as RAF (Cadet) College on November 1 1919, the college was given 'Command' status when it opened under the command of Air Commodore C. A. H. Longcroft on February 5 1920. His message, to the first entry of cadets, left no doubt as to what the service expected from its future officers: *"We have to learn by experience how to organise and administer a great Service, both in peace and war, and you, who are present at the College in its first year, will, in future, be at the helm. Therefore, you will have to work your hardest, both as cadets at the College and subsequently as officers, in order to be capable of guiding this great Service through its early days and maintaining its traditions and efficiency in the years to come."*

Among the many Cranwell graduates was Sir Frank Whittle, who attended the College during the late 1920s where he perfected his theories for the jet engine. It was appropriate that the first flight of the Gloster E.28/39, powered by his jet engine, also took place at Cranwell, on May 15 1941. The Prince of Wales, later King Edward VIII, opened the main college building in October 1934. At various times, the college has been transferred between Training, Flying, and Support Commands, and became part of Personnel and Training Command on April 1 1994.

Royal Air Force Apprentice Scheme

One of Trenchard's legacies, was that of an RAF apprentice scheme. The Apprenticeship Scheme was launched in October 1919, when candidates attended entrance examinations that were held in various centres around the country. The 1st Entry comprised a total of 235 boys who began their three-year course on January 1920 at Cranwell. This was the temporary home for the Apprentices while their permanent

accommodation was being built at Halton, in Buckinghamshire. The apprentices were signed on for a period of 12 years regular service, from the age of 18. For some, this engagement was actually closer to 15 years in total, as many were barely 15 years old, the minimum age, on joining. The youthfulness of some of the boys gave rise to the nickname 'Brats' that was given to apprentices by those in the 'Mens' service.

As well as being trained in one of the Fitter, Sheet Metal Worker, Electrical or Carpenter trades, they also underwent a course of educational study alongside military training. Many of the apprentices went on to form the nucleus of the technical command structure, and some were selected for officer training after graduating as apprentice tradesmen. Apprentices from foreign and Commonwealth air forces also trained at Halton. Over the years, there were changes in the trade courses offered to apprentices as new technologies were introduced into the world of military

RIGHT
May 1946: Lewis, a long-haired Welsh mountain goat mascot at RAF Halton is being readied for parade. After this wash and shampoo, his horns and hoofs will be gilded and he will don his specially tailored red jacket with flight sergeant's rank badges and the gold RAF crest on each side.

BELOW
Air Vice-Marshal R L R Atcherley talking to a Pakistani apprentice during a parade inspection at RAF Halton.

aviation. These included the introduction of Radio, Radar and Avionics trades, as well as a new level of Technician Apprentice during the 1960s. The Technician Apprentice trade was introduced in response to a perceived requirement for diagnostics-capable tradesmen for employment on the new aircraft types that were scheduled to enter service, including the ill-fated TSR2. There was also a degree of assimilation 'overlap' training, covering some basic electrical and associated trades knowledge, as the boundaries between the traditional single trades became less well defined than previously. The Apprenticeship Scheme came to an end with the graduation of the 155th Entry in 1993. During the 71 years of apprentice training more than 35,000 aircraft apprentices graduated from the scheme. In more recent times RAF Halton has become the School of Recruit Training, a role that retains the spirit of Trenchard.

Flying Training Schools

The Central Flying School (CFS) is the longest serving flying school in the world having been formed at Upavon, Wiltshire on May 12 1912. Initially formed as a joint service flying training school for the RFC and RNAS, its first commandant was Captain Godfrey Paine RN, who, as Commodore Paine, was later to command the The Royal Naval Air Service Central Training Establishment at Cranwell, the precursor of the Royal Air Force College. Captain Paine had learned to fly in only two weeks, at the RNAS base at Eastchurch, in order to take up this command.

Initially, the role of the CFS was to train pilots, who could already fly, in the skills necessary to become proficient military fliers. Only those who held a Royal Aero Club Certificate were accepted for training, some receiving a refund for part of their expenses incurred in obtaining the requisite certificate. As well as actual flying skills, the pilots underwent training in map reading, military

history, and practical work including engine and airframe repair. Among the successful graduates from the first course at CFS were Trenchard himself, and his future second-in-command of the Royal Air Force, Sir John Salmond.

In 1920, CFS became the Flying Instructors School and was given the task of carrying on the work started at the School of Special Flying at Gosport, where the training of instructors was carried out, along with the development of standardisation techniques and specialised flying

BELOW
Officers attending the first course at the newly established Central Flying School at Upavon, Wiltshire, 1912. Far right, middle row is Hugh Trenchard, who later became the first Marshal of the Royal Air Force.

skills. Like most formations within the Royal Air Force, the CFS was transferred between commands and stations, and renamed on several occasions, until its disbandment in 1942. It reformed in 1946, at Little Rissington, Gloucestershire, and has remained in service until the present day. Its HQ Unit was relocated to Cranwell in 1976, while some specialised units are located elsewhere, remaining under the CFS nameplate.

More flying training schools were created to train aircrew for particular flying roles within the service as needed. In the period prior to WW2, the training of aircrew to operational standards was carried out on the squadrons. This resulted in operational pilots becoming instructors on an 'ad hoc' basis, and was clearly not an effective or efficient use of resources. With the advent of WW2, it was decided to concentrate the operational training of crews within dedicated Operational Training Units. This task is broadly reflected in the modern day Tactical Weapons Unit and Operational Conversion Unit.

Chapter Three

Early Overseas Operations

RIGHT
RAF personnel embarking for Mesopotamia in 1923.

BELOW
Airmen aboard a train en-route for overseas posting.

BELOW RIGHT
Surplus SE5A fighters formed part of the Imperial Gift that led to the establishment of Commonwealth air forces.

Before the formation of the Royal Air Force in 1918, British forces had already been engaged in aerial operations in Europe and the Middle East. Units of the RFC and RNAS had been involved in operations in Belgium and France, while there were others in Palestine, Egypt, Mesopotamia, Italy and India, where No. 31 Squadron of the RFC had been based since 1915.

The Trenchard Memorandum that formed the basis for the White Paper of December 1919 had recognised the need for the overseas deployment of Royal Air Force aircraft and personnel to assist in the protection of British interests. The paper stipulated the requirement for eight squadrons and a support depot in India, seven squadrons and a depot in Egypt, and a further three squadrons and a depot in Mesopotamia. These land-based aircraft

were supplemented with three flights of seaplanes, one based in Malta, one in Alexandria, Egypt, and one on an aircraft carrier in the Mediterranean.

Wearing their newly acquired pith helmets, the airmen of the post WW1 period set off en-route to their new postings overseas. Compared with modern times, the journey to their new station was an adventure in itself, often taking several weeks to travel to places that can be reached in a few hours nowadays. The troopship, and its Army-imposed discipline, became familiar territory to airmen and officers alike, as they journeyed to places that many had previously only read about.

In May 1919, a decision was made by the War Cabinet that up to one hundred of the surplus aircraft from the Royal Air Force inventory should be gifted to countries of the British Empire and her Dominions, and also to British Colonies and Protectorates who requested them. The aircraft types ranged from deHavilland DH9 bombers and Royal Aircraft Factory SE5A fighters, to Avro

504 trainers. Known as the Imperial Gift, this act led to the subsequent creation of air forces in Australia, Canada and South Africa.

Russia, Afghanistan and Iraq

Following the armistice that ended action in World War I, there was a continuing British military involvement in the aftermath of the Russian revolution.

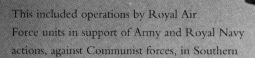

This included operations by Royal Air Force units in support of Army and Royal Navy actions, against Communist forces, in Southern

Russia and the Black Sea. RAF units taking part were No. 17 Squadron with DH9s, and No. 47 Squadron with Sopwith Camels, along with carrier-based Short 184 seaplanes of No. 286 Squadron.

In May 1919, after the outbreak of the Third Afghan War, No. 31 Squadron was involved in raids on the Afghan city of Jelalabad, with the loss of three aircraft. After a bombing campaign by the Royal Air Force in which leaflets giving warning of the impending action had first been dropped on Afghan towns and villages, in an attempt to avoid unnecessary civilian casualties, the Third Afghan War came to an end in August 1919.

One of the more intriguing connections between the Royal Air Force and the Middle East began in 1922, when a certain John Hume Ross enlisted in the RAF. Transferring to the Tank Corps in 1923, and changing his name to Thomas Edward Shaw, the man that was the famed 'Lawrence of Arabia' eventually reverted to the RAF, and served thereafter as Aircraftsman T.E. Shaw. First based at Drigh Road in Karachi in 1927, he was later posted to Peshawar, and then to the border town of Miranshah, in Waziristan, near to the Afghanistan border, that was the smallest RAF station in India at that time. Lawrence's presence in the area was the subject of many

BELOW
Aircraftsman T.E.Shaw outside his billet somewhere in the Middle East.

MAIN
RAF Westland Wapiti
aircraft in formation
over Iraq in 1935.

postulations, some believing that his service in the Royal Air Force was a cover for clandestine operations. This belief was given further credence when, in September 1928, rumours spread that he was 'spying for Britain', in Afghanistan, while disguised as a Moslem spiritual guide. An uprising against King Amanullah in Afghanistan, in December 1928, that resulted in the abdication of Amanullah in the following January fuelled these suspicions, causing Lawrence (Aircraftsman Shaw) to be recalled to Britain.

In an insight into life in the Royal Air Force in the 1920s, Shaw (writing under the name of T.E. Lawrence) in his book The Mint, describes his observations on the attitudes of other airmen towards RAF ex-apprentices in the following extract:

"But there is rising up a second category of airman, the boy apprentice. The boys come fresh from school, glib in theory, essay writers, with the bench tricks of workmen. An old rigger, with years of service, finds himself in charge of a boy-beginner with twice his pay. The kid is clever with words, and has passed out L.A.C. from school: the old hand can hardly spell, and will forever be an AC2. He teaches his better ever so grumpily. Nor do all the ex-boys make the job easier for those they are about to replace. As a class they are cocky. Remember how we enlisted men have been cowed. The

airmen of the future will not be so owned by their service. Rather, they will be the service, maintaining it, and their rights in it, as one with the officers. In the old days, men had to strip off their boots and socks, and expose their feet for an officer's inspection. The ex-boys'd kick you in the teeth."

Shaw had, presumably, never been in a situation whereby 'boy apprentices' were forced to expose somewhat more than their bare feet for inspection, by officers, in the ritual known as the FFI (Free From Infection) inspection. Although a medical officer carried out the actual physical inspection, the FFI procedure usually took place with the apprentices 'Standing-by their Beds' as a parade, on a par with a full kit inspection. On a word of command, the embarrassed assembly, in unison, were ordered to lower their 'drawers, cellular', (or the equivalent under-garment of the day), thus exposing themselves not only to the medical officer and his orderly, but also to the gaze of the 'chain of command' entourage that accompanied him.

Air Control and Colonial Policing

One of the policies advocated by Trenchard, as a means of securing British interests overseas, by suppressing uprisings from the air, with less personnel and at lower cost, became known as Air Control. First used successfully against the 'Mad Mullah' and his supporters in Somaliland in 1920, where the vast expanses of territory made

Chapter Three

operations solely by ground troops difficult and time-consuming, it was not long before the policy of Air Control was introduced elsewhere.

Trenchard proposed that the Royal Air Force be given full responsibility for conducting military operations in Britain's most troublesome new mandate, the former Ottoman provinces of Mesopotamia, that formed part of modern Iraq. The Trenchard paper asserted that the RAF could police the mandate with aircraft squadrons and some armoured-car squadrons, supported by a small number of British and locally-recruited troops, at a fraction of the cost of a large army garrison.

The financial benefit to the Exchequer, as well as the military strategy, was readily accepted within the corridors of power in Whitehall, and the proposal agreed. By October 1922, Air Marshal John Salmond assumed direct overall command, together with military responsibility for Iraq, on behalf of the British government. The RAF initially deployed a force comprising eight squadrons of fighters and light bombers, including the DH9 reconnaissance/light bomber and the Vickers Vernon troop-transport/bomber. The Air Control policy worked to such effect that, throughout the 1929s and 1930s, the situation in Iraq was kept largely under control by bombing, or sometimes by simply over-flying, the troublesome elements.

The effectiveness of Air Control was further emphasised in 1925, when Nos. 5, 27 and 60 Squadrons were sent to operate their Bristol Fighters and DH9s from airfields at Miranshah and Tank, in order to control the Mahsud tribesmen in

South Waziristan. Carrying out air operations including an air blockade and offensive actions against mountain strongholds, the campaign known as 'Pink's War', after Wing Commander R.C.M. Pink who commanded the Royal Air Force units, was successfully concluded within two months. The operation was completed with the loss of one aircraft and its crew, and without the use of ground troops.

Policing of its territories, largely by the use of air power, became commonplace throughout the British Empire. Bombing raids replaced the traditional Army ground operations that had previously been mounted against dissidents on the Northwest Frontier in India, and elsewhere. The

LEFT
Signboard outside the RAF base in Iraq that was built in the 1920s.

RIGHT
Habbaniyah 2006. U.S. soldier outside former RAF accommodation block dating from the 1920s. Note the addition of air conditioning units and new roofing.

BELOW LEFT
RAF armoured cars and Vimy bomber in Mesopotamia, 1922.

policy worked to great effect in the Aden Protectorate, where aircraft were used on numerous occasions to deal swiftly with trouble in the interior.

The Far East

In 1927, Royal Air Force units formed part of a tri-service deployment to Shanghai that was tasked to protect European nationals, and their property, from Chinese Communist forces. Subsequently, a headquarters was established in Hong Kong, as Royal Air Force China Command, thereby establishing a connection with the Far East that would be retained for many years, albeit not continuously. At the end of May 1927, No. 2 Squadron, equipped with Bristol F2B aircraft, arrived in Shanghai to reinforce China Command. They remained in Shanghai until the threat had diminished sufficiently for Royal Air Force China Command to be disbanded, before returning to Britain in October of that year.

The first major RAF organisation to be established in the Far East was set up in Singapore, in 1930, to control all Royal Air Force assets in South East Asia. The headquarters was located in Singapore and was known as Royal Air Force Base Singapore, until 1933, when it became

Headquarters Air Force Far East Command. The Royal Air Force continued to serve in India and Iraq, the Middle East and Far East, and on the African continent, throughout the 1920s and 1930s. Many squadrons received Battle Honours, belatedly promulgated in February 1947, that reflected their participation in many 'Local' wars. However, these honours were not eligible for inclusion on Squadron Standards.

ROYAL AIR FORCE BATTLE HONOURS

1919 – 1939

Aden 1928, 1929, 1934
Afghanistan 1919-1920, Burma 1930-1932
Iraq 1919-1920, 1923-1925, 1928-1929
Kurdistan 1919, 1922-1925, 1930-1931
Mahsud 1919-1920, Mohmand 1927, 1933
Northern Kurdistan 1932
Northern Russia 1918-1919
North West Frontier 1930-1931, 1935-1939
North West Persia 1920, Palestine 1936-1939
Somaliland 1920, South Persia 1918-1919
South Russia 1919-1920, Sudan 1920
Transjordan 1924, Waziristan 1919-1925

Long Distance Flights and Record Attempts

During the immediate post-World War I years, and throughout the 1920s and 1930s, there were many notable flights undertaken by Royal Air Force personnel. These flights were often made for reasons of publicity, as a means of waving the flag for both Britain and its newly formed air force, or to demonstrate the practicality of military reinforcement, by air, throughout the British Empire. In a time of post-war defence cuts, there had been some lobbying by the War Office and the Admiralty, with support from some government ministers, who felt that the 'junior' service should revert to a lesser role under the two, more senior, armed services. This notion was strongly resisted by the members of the Air Council. Part of the Royal Air Force's opposition to the Army and Navy lobbying involved the demonstration of the capabilities of aircraft to travel over long distances, and at significantly higher speeds than surface transport could attain, in the defence and protection of British interests overseas.

One of the most notable of the early long distance flying achievements was that of Major A. MacLaren, when he piloted a Handley Page V/1500 bomber 'Old Carthusian' from England to India. Taking off on December 13 1918, he finally landed in Delhi just over one month later. This particular aircraft subsequently took part in operations in Afghanistan where, on May 24 1919, it bombed the city of Kabul.

On June 14-15 1919, Captain John Alcock and Lieutenant Arthur Whitten Brown made the first non-stop flight across the Atlantic when they flew from St John's, in Newfoundland, to Clifden in County Galway, Ireland, in a modified Vickers

Vimy bomber. Their total flight time was 16 hours 27 minutes, and ended in an ignominious crash landing in a boggy field. Both men were later knighted in recognition of their Trans-Atlantic achievement. Just a few weeks later, on July 6, the Royal Air Force airship R34 arrived in New

MAIN
Airship R34 landing at Pulham, Norfolk after completing the first two-way crossing of the Atlantic in 1919.

York, thus completing the first crossing of the Atlantic by an airship, having departed from East Fortune in Scotland on July 2nd. Under the command of Major G.H. Scott, the R34 with its crew of 30 RAF and U.S. Navy personnel, then commenced the return journey on July 9, and landed, at Pulham in Norfolk, four days later.

In September 1927, the Royal Air Force took part in the Schneider Trophy competition in Venice, Italy, where a Supermarine S5 seaplane, flown by Flight Lieutenant S.N. Webster, won the race at an average speed of 281 mph. The same aircraft set a closed circuit record of 283 mph over a distance of 100 kilometres. Despite winning the race, there was great opposition from within both the government and, unbelievably, the Air Ministry, before they both gave some ground, and permitted the participation in the defence of the Trophy in the 1929 race at Cowes. This resulted in the Schneider Trophy being won for the second time by the Royal Air Force High Speed Flight, with a Supermarine S6 seaplane piloted by Flight Lieutenant H.R.D. Waghorn, at an average speed of 328mph. The engine for this aircraft had been privately funded by Rolls-Royce, due to the reluctance of the Air Ministry to finance the building of '…a military engine with racing capabilities': R.J.Mitchell, who was later responsible for the design of the Spitfire fighter, designed the S6 aircraft.

The period leading up to the 1931 Schneider Trophy races was full of political and military opposition to the continued involvement of the RAF. The government's view was that participation by the Royal Air Force '…was not in accordance with the spirit of a sporting event…' and which might '…not inconceivably lead to

diplomatic incidents.' The Air Ministry objected to the use of its pilots on the grounds that any publicity given to the team would adversely affect morale within the Service. Even Sir Hugh Trenchard voiced his objections, saying that he could see '…nothing of value in it…' as he believed that high-speed aircraft could be developed without the distraction, and expense, of the Schneider Trophy competition. Together with a donation of some £100,000 pounds from Lady Lucy Houston, the widow of a wealthy shipping owner, British participation was ensured after the government relented, and allowed the RAF to defend the trophy for a second time. This defence was successful as the race, over the Solent, was won by Flt. Lt. J.N. Boothman in a Supermarine S6B seaplane powered by a 2,300hp Rolls-Royce 'R-Type' engine, at an average speed of 340.08 mph, thus winning the Schneider Trophy outright.

RIGHT
The outright winners of the Schneider Trophy pictured in front of a Supermarine S6B, August 1931. From left to right; Flight Lieutenant Hope, Lieutenant G.L. Brinton, Flight Lieutenant W. Long, Flight Lieutenant G.H. Stainforth, Squadron Leader Orlebar, Flight Lieutenant J.N. Boothman, Flying Officer L.S. Snaith and Flight Lieutenant Dry.

Chapter Four

Conflict on the Horizon

At the beginning of the new decade, and throughout the 1930s, the Royal Air Force continued to be involved in the series of 'Little Wars' and colonial policing operations in Africa and the Middle East, in particular, the ongoing operations in Afghanistan and Iraq.

In 1932, in support of Iraqi troops fighting against a small-scale revolt in north-east Iraq that was instigated by Sheikh Ahmad of Barzan, bombing raids by Royal Air Force aircraft were sometimes preceded by leaflet drops warning villages of the forthcoming attacks, in an attempt to minimise collateral casualties. One of the earliest uses of aerial broadcasts by the Royal Air Force against ground forces occurred during this campaign, when verbal warnings were given, in Kurdish dialect, using a loudspeaker system fitted to a Vickers Victoria transport aircraft. The subsequent bombing raids by aircraft from Nos. 30, 55 and 70 Squadrons led to the surrender of the dissidents.

The use of aircraft as the means of transporting troops, rapidly, between theatres of operations was demonstrated to great effect in 1932. On this occasion, the 1st Battalion of the Northamptonshire Regiment was flown from Ismailia, in Egypt, to Hinaidi in Iraq, aboard the Vickers Victorias of No. 70 Squadron, Iraq

BELOW
Royal Air Force
Westland Wapiti
aircraft flying over
rugged landscape of
Iraq in 1934.

Command, and No. 216 Squadron, Middle East Command.

Meanwhile, at home in Britain, in addition to winning the Schneider Trophy, the Royal Air Force was kept in the public eye with a series of Air Pageants at Hendon that had first taken place in 1920. These were spectacular displays, involving many different types of aircraft carrying out parachuting, formation flying and aerobatics demonstrations, and usually culminated in a mock bombing attack on a specially constructed 'enemy'

stronghold. Empire Air Days, the first of which took place in 1934, were held annually at civilian aerodromes, as well as at various RAF stations where the proceeds were donated to the Royal Air Force Benevolent Fund.

The 1936 event at Henlow was attended by 8,414 visitors, and the sum of £23 15s 11d was raised for the Fund. The air shows became so popular that, by 1939, no fewer than 5 civilian aerodromes and 63 RAF stations were open to the public.

LEFT
RAF Air Pageant in
1930 at Hendon
Aerodrome, now the
site of the Royal Air
Force Museum.

In celebration of the Silver Jubilee of King George V, on July 6 1935, a Royal Review of the Royal Air Force was held at Mildenhall and Duxford, where the King inspected 200 aircraft on the ground, and was given a flypast salute by 350 aircraft.

Organisational Changes

Within the Service, there were some organisational changes including the abolition of the rank title of Sergeant-Major, in favour of that of Warrant Officer, in 1933. On the operational side, the squadron system was introduced for Fleet Air Arm units. Since its formation in 1924, the Fleet Air Arm had consisted of a number of 'Flights', each of which had normally comprised six aircraft. In 1933, these Flights were reformed into squadrons, each having a complement of between nine and twelve aircraft, and allocated a squadron number in the 800 series. The changes in Fleet Air Arm structure were in place for a period of only four years before the Branch was returned to Admiralty control, under the Royal Navy, in 1937.

A series of major changes to the organisation of the Royal Air Force took place in 1936. The Air Defence of Great Britain (ADGB) command, responsible for Home defence fighter and bomber forces that was created in 1925, was abolished. Created in its place were Fighter Command, Bomber Command and Coastal Command, as well as a new Training Command that took over the previously independent 'command status' training units at Cranwell and Halton. The King's Flight was officially created in the same year, as was the Royal Air Force Volunteer Reserve (RAFVR). The RAFVR was created with the intention of recruiting around 800 trainee pilots, 2,500 observers, and 5,200 wireless operator/air gunners between 1936 and 1938. These target numbers were increased as the international situation

deteriorated. In December, the Royal Air Force Officers Engineering Course, at RAF Henlow, was renamed the Royal Air Force School of Aeronautical Engineering.

Also in 1936, the Balloon Barrage scheme was announced. Balloon barrages were intended to deter low-level attacks on important installations by forcing hostile aircraft to fly above the balloons, thus restricting the accuracy of hostile bombers and, at the same time, expose them to anti-aircraft fire for longer periods. Later, in 1938, Maintenance Command was formed at Andover, the first Air Defence Cadet Corps training squadron was formed at Leicester, and a Balloon Command was formed with responsibility for barrage balloons. Reacting to the Munich crisis, the Royal Air Force introduced emergency measures in preparation for war, including the establishment of Mobilisation Pools for the purpose of organising large groups of personnel and their subsequent movement drafts.

The early months of 1939 saw the formation of the Auxiliary Air Force Reserve. This was created to enable ex-members of the Auxiliary Air Force to serve with auxiliary flying squadrons in an emergency. The women's services were also augmented with the establishment of the Women's Auxiliary Air Force. Reserve Command was also formed in this year but the title was short-lived, as it was absorbed into Flying Training Command in the following year.

Countering the Threat

In March 1934, the Prime Minister, Stanley Baldwin, had given an assurance to the House of Commons that any failure to bring about an international agreement for air disarmament, at the International Disarmament Conference, would result in the British Government taking steps to raise the strength of the Royal Air Force. This increase would be such that it would have the resources to equal those of the '…strongest air force within striking distance of the United Kingdom.' Initial provision was for the establishment of six new squadrons. By July 1934, the Cabinet had approved the first Royal Air Force Expansion Scheme, known as Expansion Scheme 'A'. This provided for the increase in strength of the Royal Air Force to that of 111 front-line squadrons, at home and overseas, totalling around 1,252 aircraft. This provision, together with an increase in Fleet Air Arm numbers to 16 squadrons totalling some 213 aircraft, by March 31 1939 was considered to be sufficient to counter any foreseeable threat from Germany. As a consequence, there was little provision for reserves. Meanwhile, in Germany, there was a continuing build-up of military strength, leading to the formation of the Reichsluftwaffe in March 1935, in contravention of the terms of the Treaty of Versailles. Two months later, the title was abbreviated to become 'Luftwaffe'. In the same month, the British Government announced a further increase in the strength of the Royal Air Force, to 1,500 aircraft, by 1937.

The growing threat to peace was heightened by the invasion in 1935 of Abyssinia, by Italy, from its bases in Eritrea and Somaliland. Britain responded by sending military reinforcements to the Mediterranean and the Middle East, including 11 Royal Air Force squadrons, where they remained until the late summer of 1936. That same year, a series of air defence exercises were held in Britain. For the purposes of the exercises it was assumed, correctly, as was later proved, that enemy forces would enter British airspace over the coast of south-east England. The exercises also served to test the effectiveness of the Observer Corps that was founded in 1925. The Corps had been under the control of the Army until 1929, when it passed to the Air Ministry in order to provide closer collaboration with the air defence organisation.

In June 1939, as the political situation in Europe continued to worsen, the Secretary of State for Air, Sir Kingsley Wood, announced that the Royal Air Force would impress civil aircraft into service in the event of war. During the summer of that year, Bomber Command took part in a series of navigational exercises over Central and Southern France, that were for both 'training' and 'show of strength' purposes, involving around

MAIN
Members of the
Royal Observer
Corps survey the
skies over the South
Coast of England.

240 aircraft. Further exercises took place, including small-scale operations with French Air Force units, that culminated in a final 'practice' in which over 1,300 aircraft participated.

Concrete Ears and Radar Eyes

One of the major shortcomings in Britain's defences was the lack of advance warning of enemy air attack. Air exercises, that were held to test the country's defences, demonstrably illustrated the ineffectiveness of both the current defensive equipment, and the procedures in use at the time. More than half of the bombers reached their exercise targets unopposed, and in many cases undetected, even though their routes and targets were known in advance. The Prime Minister, Stanley Baldwin, had previously stated, "The bomber will always get through": his prophecy was not too far away from being true.

The Army had been experimenting with an acoustic detection system that, it was proposed,

would give sufficient advance warning of enemy aircraft to allow its guns to engage their targets. The system utilised a massive concrete parabolic reflector, with a microphone at its focal point, to pick up the sound of approaching aircraft. Unfortunately, the system also picked up other sounds that were not made by aircraft, thus rendering it almost useless in anything other than near-silent ambient conditions.

Resulting from the failures of acoustic detection equipment and methods, the Air Ministry set out to rectify the situation. They immediately instituted a review that led to the involvement of Robert Watson-Watt, as Superintendent of the Radio Research Station at

MAIN
Heyford bomber as used in air exercises in the thirties.

Slough, initially to carry out feasibility studies into the possibilities of using radio waves to damage an aircraft, or incapacitate its pilot. While this was discovered to be impractical, the radio energy that was reflected from an aircraft could be detected at 'useful' ranges. To demonstrate the viability of the theory, Watson-Watt and his team used powerful short wave transmissions from the BBC transmitter station at Daventry, and measured the signals reflected from a Royal Air Force Heyford bomber. Detection ranges of up to eight miles were achieved, leading to further funding and, within a few months, ranges of 40 miles were being reliably

achieved. By August 1936, the first station was in operation at Bawdsey and a further four, located in a chain around the coast, shortly afterwards.

Plots of incoming aircraft were passed by telephone to a central operations room, where the information could be co-ordinated with visual sighting reports received from the Royal Observer Corps, and data from the radio direction-finding system. Using the combined data, Royal Air Force personnel based at Biggin Hill developed fighter control and interception techniques that were considered to be effective for daytime use against larger groups of aircraft, but not against smaller, dispersed groups, at night. This led to experiments with the object of testing airborne versions of the system. Initial tests, again using a Heyford bomber, gave detection ranges of over ten miles. The airborne system proved effective in poor weather conditions, as well as against surface ships, at several miles range. These initial trials led to the further development of Air Interception (AI) and Air to Surface Vessel (ASV) equipment, and the construction of Chain Low (CHL) stations, to detect low-flying intruders, around the coasts of Britain. All of these developments were to prove vital to the defence of the country in the coming years.

Whittle and the Jet Engine

Frank Whittle applied to join the RAF as an apprentice, at the age of 16 years, in January 1923. After passing the entrance examination, he was initially rejected, on the grounds of his small stature. With the persistence that was to stand him in good stead later in his service career, and following an intensive fitness program, he re-applied six months later, and was accepted. On successful completion of his apprenticeship, he was offered a cadetship to the RAF College, Cranwell where he trained as a pilot.

While at Cranwell, Whittle wrote a thesis exploring the possibilities of flight at higher altitudes and speeds than could be achieved by contemporary aircraft. He expounded the potential of both rocket propulsion and the gas turbine, the latter possibly to be used to drive a ducted propeller, or fan. The concept of pure jet propulsion was not formulated until the year after he left Cranwell. However, the Air Ministry was not impressed, believing that the gas turbine was impracticable, but Whittle, undeterred, took out a patent in 1930. After graduation from Cranwell, Whittle was posted to a fighter squadron at Hornchurch, followed by duties at the Flying

BELOW
Group Captian Frank Whittle, inventor of the jet engine, pictured at his desk in 1944.

Training School at Digby, before becoming a float-plane test pilot at the Marine Aircraft Experimental Establishment, Felixstowe. He later attended the Officers' School of Engineering at Henlow where, in 1934, he graduated with exceptional results. This led to him entering Cambridge University, as an undergraduate in Mechanical Sciences.

With support from friends who had arranged financial backing from a London bank, Whittle began construction of his first engine in 1935. This engine, which had a single-stage centrifugal compressor coupled to a single-stage turbine, was first run in April 1937. Although it was simply a test rig, and not intended for use in an aircraft, it successfully demonstrated the feasibility of the turbojet concept. After negotiations with, by now, a more receptive Air Ministry, a company called Power Jets Ltd was formed. Whittle was allotted shares in return for assigning all his patent rights to the company. A contract for the design of an experimental bench engine, the 'WU', was awarded to the British Thomson Houston Company, at Rugby. After gaining his first class honours degree at Cambridge, Whittle was granted a further post-graduate year to supervise the work on the WU engine, which made its first run on April 12 1937.

Whittle was appointed to the Special Duty List and continued to work for Power Jets as Honorary Chief Engineer. By June 1939, the work had progressed sufficiently for the Air Ministry to place an order for a flight engine, the W.1, with the company. The Gloster Aircraft Company was contracted to build an experimental aircraft, the E.28/39, which was to be powered by the W.1. The highly successful first test flights of the E.28/39, on May 15 1941, resulted in an expansion of the project, and the beginning of co-operation between Britain and the USA on the development of the turbo-jet engine. Before the outcome of the test flights, a decision was taken to build a twin-engine fighter, the Gloster F.9/40 (Meteor), using the more powerful W.2.B engine. In 1944, the Meteor entered service and was the only Allied jet to be operational in World War Two. Before his attachment to Power Jets ended in 1946, Whittle was also responsible for the development of the W2/500 and the W2/700 engines, the parents of subsequent Rolls-Royce engines.

Out with the Old, and in with the New

In the 1920s, although there were numerous occasions where RAF aircraft had been used in military operations, these had usually been against ground forces and installations or, for transporting troops. By the early 1930s, the inventory of Royal Air Force aircraft largely comprised a series of outdated bombers and transports. Most of these were modified versions of aeroplanes that had either been developed towards the end of World War I or, were completed too late to have taken part in that event. The biplane aircraft was in its prime; however, it would not be long before new developments in construction methods and materials, as well as design innovations, would signal the start of a new era in aircraft design.

Although not supported with great enthusiasm by the government or the Air Ministry at the time, the successful winning of the Schneider Trophy had proved to be of much greater worth than was mooted by the more sceptical commentators of the day. It would be several years before the investment made by the British aircraft industry and the Royal Air Force High Speed Flight, in winning the Schneider Trophy, would be proved to have been worthwhile. In the meantime, the biplane continued to form the mainstay of the RAF front-line aircraft catalogue. Included in this category was a varied assortment of flying machines, some pleasing to the eye, others less than attractive to the purist. Falling into the 'less than attractive' classification were aircraft such as the Handley Page Hinaidi twin-engine bomber that was in operational service between 1929 and 1933. The Hinaidi was an improved version of the 1923-vintage Hyderabad from the same manufacturer, and served with Nos. 10, 99 and 503 Squadrons. Some were converted to

RIGHT
Bristol Bulldog planes being constructed at Filton.

BELOW
Hawker Hart light bomber circa 1930.

troop transport aircraft, and used extensively throughout the Middle East.

The most numerous fighter aircraft of the Royal Air Force, in the early 1930s, was the Bristol Bulldog that had entered service in 1929. This biplane fighter was fitted with a Bristol Jupiter engine, and was capable of speeds of almost 180 miles per hour, with a range of some 300 miles. Armed with two 0.303-inch machine guns, it could also carry four 20-pound bombs. One of its main attributes was that, apart from being an excellent aeroplane, it was relatively economical to operate and maintain, an important feature in times of constrained defence budgets.

Among the more aesthetically pleasing aircraft types of the biplane era were those produced by the Hawker Company. The Hawker series of military biplanes were evolutions of the Sopwith aircraft of World War I. In the late 1920s, following the introduction of the Rolls Royce V12 'F-series' engine that was the forerunner of the famous Kestrel, together with the development of metal airframe structures, the Hawker Company produced the sleek and beautiful Fury fighter, and the Hart two-seater light-bomber and training aircraft. The Fury was a direct predecessor of the Hurricane; the Hart led to many variants, including the Hind and the Audax that were in

BELOW
Loading live bombs onto Hawker Demon, K2845, at Armament Training Camp, RAF Sutton Bridge, Lincolnshire. In the foreground are two dummy bombs used to test the release gear before fitting the live bombs.

service until the outbreak of World War II. The Hart was a particularly good aircraft, with a rapid rate of climb, and was excellent in aerobatics. Although a bomber, in 1930, it could outpace every fighter of its day.

In August 1934, the first of a batch of 12 Avro Rota Mark I autogiros entered service with the School of Army Co-operation at RAF Old Sarum, becoming the first rotary-wing aircraft to be operated by the Royal Air Force. The autogiro had been designed and developed by the Spaniard, Juan de la Cierva, who moved to Britain in the mid-1920s, and was designated Cierva C.30A. Its inventor had sold licenses for production in a number of countries, including France, Britain and Germany. The main feature of this aircraft was the fact that the rotor, which auto-rotated freely in normal flight, could also be spun-up before takeoff, thus decreasing the distance required for the autogiro to become airborne to around 90 feet. Although not capable of hovering, the

Rota could fly very slowly and, with a landing speed of around 10 miles per hour, was considered to be relatively easy to fly when compared with its successor, the helicopter. The aircraft remained in service with the RAF in a variety of roles, including radar calibration duties, until 1945.

During 1935 and 1936, several new aircraft types entered service with RAF squadrons, including the Boulton Paul Overstrand. The Overstrand was notable in that it was the last twin-engine biplane bomber to fly with the service, as well as being the first to be equipped with an enclosed, power-operated gun turret. The Short Singapore III flying boat entered service with No. 230 Squadron, and was deployed to Alexandria in 1935. Although obsolescent when delivered, the Singapore III remained in service until the early years of the coming war. Other notable debutantes of the period were the Gloster Gauntlet, Hawker

Fury II, Hawker Hind and Avro Anson. The mid-1930s were notable in that, during these years, two of the most famous fighter aircraft of World War II made their maiden flights.

On November 6 1935, the prototype of the Hawker Hurricane fighter, powered by a Rolls-Royce Merlin engine, made its first flight from Brooklands, flown by Hawker test pilot P.W.S. 'George' Bulman. When it entered service with No. 111 Squadron at Northolt, in December 1937, the Hurricane became the first monoplane fighter aircraft to be adopted by the Royal Air Force, and the first combat aircraft operated by the service that was capable of exceeding 300 miles per hour in level flight. It was also the first RAF fighter with a retractable undercarriage, as well as being the first to be armed with eight guns.

Designed by Sidney Camm, the Hurricane was based on a monoplane derivative of the Hawker Fury biplane fighter and was originally to have been powered by the Rolls-Royce Goshawk engine. With the advent of the Merlin engine, Camm re-designed his aircraft around the new power plant. The Hurricane was a traditional Hawker design that featured a tubular metal fuselage frame that was constructed with mechanically fastened joints, rather than being welded. The fuselage was covered with a fabric, similar to that of its predecessor, the Fury. Each wing was constructed with two steel spars and ribs, and was also fabric-covered. From 1939, the wing surfaces were skinned with sheet metal. Many of the aircraft's surfaces and contours, especially around the tail, bore the classic lines that were reminiscent of earlier Camm designs.

R J Mitchell, Chief Designer at Supermarine, had previously been responsible for the design of the successful Schneider Trophy-winning seaplanes in the late 1920s and early 1930s. His first fighter design in 1933, the Type 224 featured a Rolls-Royce Goshawk steam-cooled engine but was slow, and under-powered. Coupled with the unreliability of its steam engine-cooling system, it was considered unsuitable for use as an interceptor fighter in the Royal Air Force. This led to Mitchell designing a revolutionary new airframe around the Rolls-Royce PV12 engine, initially a private venture, as shown in its designation letters, that was later to become the Merlin. The new aircraft, designated F37/34 showed great potential, even while still a 'paper aeroplane' on the drawing board. Its maiden flight, on March 5 1936 at Eastleigh, near Southampton, was carried out by the chief test pilot of Vickers Supermarine, Joe 'Mutt' Summers. Although the undercarriage was locked down, and no armament had been fitted, the aircraft was more than satisfactory at this early stage. With a design calculation for a top speed of 350 miles per hour, it actually reached 349 miles per hour during trials. Together with its high

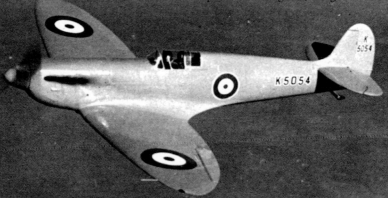

speed, excellent handling, and eight-gun armament, this aircraft was destined to go down in history as one of the greatest fighter aircraft of its era, as well as being one of great aesthetic appeal.

The forerunner of the aircraft that was to become the backbone of the RAF bomber force, in the first two years of World War II, first flew in 1936, and was originally known as the 'Crecy'. This aircraft was a smaller, unarmed version of the aircraft that first flew late in 1937. The Vickers Wellington, as it was eventually named, was popularly known as 'the Wimpy', by service personnel, after J. Wellington Wimpy, a character from the Popeye cartoons. The Wellington used a

unique geodetic-construction design similar to that used by Barnes Wallis for airships, that was also used by Vickers in the single-engine Wellesley bomber. This type of construction was extremely strong, and relatively light and easy to repair, but took longer to construct than the monocoque-system used in other aircraft. The Wellington Mk.I was powered by two 1,050 horsepower Bristol Pegasus engines, and equipped with two power-operated gun turrets. It could carry a bomb load of around 4,500 pounds. The Mk.I version first entered service with No. 9 Squadron in October 1938, and was to outlast its more numerous counterparts, the twin-engine Handley

MAIN
Aircraft and airmen of the Royal Air Force station at Heliopolis on parade, 1938.

Page Hampden, and Armstrong Whitworth Whitley bombers, in operational use.

As the end of the decade approached, the political situation in Europe continued to deteriorate. The formation of the Luftwaffe, by Germany, in blatant disregard for the terms of the Treaty of Versailles in 1918, and its subsequent involvement in the Spanish Civil War, threatened the uneasy peace that existed on the continent. Many believed that armed conflict was inevitable. Others, in particular some members of the British Government, continued a policy of appeasement. The outcome of this policy was to have a major impact on the lives of millions of people, not only in Europe, but also throughout most of the world.

After arriving at Croydon Airport, in September 1938, the Prime Minister Neville Chamberlain held aloft a sheet of paper that had been signed by himself and the German Chancellor, Adolf Hitler, which he believed to be the key to a peaceful Europe. In his speech Chamberlain said, *"My good friends, for the second time in our history, a British Prime Minister has returned from Germany bringing peace with honour. I believe it is peace for our time."*

His belief was to be confounded in less than one year.

Chapter Five

Their Finest Hour

Declaration of War

In January 1939, the Royal Air Force operational aircraft inventory consisted of 135 squadrons in total: 74 bomber, 27 fighter, 12 army co-operation, 17 reconnaissance, 4 torpedo-bomber, and 1 communications squadron. At the same time, the strength of the Auxiliary Air Force totalled 19 squadrons: 3 bomber, 11 fighter, 2 army co-operation, and 3 reconnaissance squadrons.

In March 1939, Hitler's troops invaded Czechoslovakia. Britain was forced to abandon its stance in appeasing Hitler, and warned Germany that any further attacks would be met with force. Six months later, German forces invaded Poland. The British and French governments both declared war against Germany on the same day, September 3 1939. The Prime Minister, Neville Chamberlain, gave the news in a radio broadcast to the British nation. The message contained the chilling statement, *"This morning the British Ambassador in Berlin handed the German Government a final note stating that, unless we hear from them by 11 o'clock that they were prepared at once to withdraw their troops from Poland, a state of war would exist between us. I have to tell you now that no such undertaking has been received, and that consequently this country is at war with Germany."*

On the same night, seven Whitley bombers of No. 58 Squadron, and three from No. 51

BELOW
Loading propaganda leaflets onto a Whitley bomber in early 1940.

Squadron, dropped propaganda leaflets over Germany. Nearly six million copies of the leaflet carrying the text of a message headed 'Warning! A Message from Britain' were dropped over Bremen, Hamburg, and the Ruhr. The following night a further three million leaflets were dropped and, during the first month of the war, more than twenty million leaflets, with five different messages, were discharged over enemy territory.

The first year of the war, otherwise known as the 'phoney war' because of the comparative lack of any significant military action in Europe, was noted for the large number of these leaflet raids carried out by the RAF. One result of these raids was that the Germans stepped up their anti-aircraft batteries, thus making life more hazardous for those on subsequent missions. Some politicians believed that the raids served a purpose. Many military leaders held the opposite view, including 'Bomber' Harris, Commander-in-Chief of RAF Bomber Command from 1942-45, who later stated, *"My personal view is that the only thing*

Chapter Five

achieved was largely to supply the continent's requirements of toilet paper for the five long years of the war."

Operations Commence

On the day that war was declared, a Bristol Blenheim IV aircraft, serial number N6215, of No. 139 Squadron at Wyton, became the first Royal Air Force aircraft to enter German airspace. The aircraft was captained by Flying Officer A. McPherson, who was later awarded the Distinguished Flying Cross (DFC), and carried out a visual and photographic reconnaissance of German naval ports and shipping.

The Royal Air Force's first offensive sorties of the Second World War also took place on the opening day, September 3 1939, when eighteen Handley Page Hampdens, and nine Vickers Wellingtons, of Bomber Command took part in an operation against German naval shipping. On this occasion, they failed to locate any targets, and returned to base. This first day of war saw the first RAF casualty when Pilot Officer John Noel Isaac, of No. 600 Squadron, became the first British serviceman to die in the war. His Bristol Blenheim crashed into Heading Street, in Hendon, at 1250hrs, less than two hours after the declaration of war.

The war was to last only one day for Sergeant George Booth, an observer with No. 107 Squadron. On September 4, his Blenheim aircraft was shot down over the German coast and, although he survived the attack, he was captured and, thereby, earned the dubious distinction of becoming the first member of the Royal Air Force to become a prisoner of war.

This same day also saw a concerted bomber attack on German warships at Wilhelmshafen, Brunsbüttel, and the Schillig Roads. Fourteen Wellingtons, from No. 9 and No. 149 Squadrons, and fifteen Bristol Blenheims, of Nos. 107, 110 and 139 Squadrons, took part in the raid. Ten Blenheims from Nos. 107 and 110 Squadrons attacked the pocket battleship Admiral Scheer, at Wilhelmshafen, and scored three hits, but the bombs failed to detonate. In the attack on the cruiser Emden, in the same port, there was a bizarre coincidence when a Blenheim piloted by a pilot with the same name as the target vessel, Flying Officer H.L. Emden, crashed onto the deck, killing its crew of four. Seventeen aircrew failed to return from this mission. Its leader, Flight Lieutenant KC Doran of No. 110 Squadron received the DFC for his part in the operation.

Following the first raids by the Luftwaffe over Britain on September 6, there followed an instance of 'blue

MAIN
Bristol Blenheim
IV light bomber,
circa 1940.

on blue' that had tragic consequences. A technical fault at the 'Chain Home' radar direction finding station at Canewdon, in Essex, together with errors made within the Fighter Command control system, resulted in friendly aircraft being

incorrectly identified as an incoming air raid. Hurricane fighters from No. 56 Squadron at North Weald, that were 'scrambled' to intercept the supposed raiders, were also identified as hostile. Further squadrons were then scrambled and, amid the confusion, a section of Spitfires from No. 74 Squadron at Hornchurch mistakenly identified two of the Hurricanes as being

Messerschmitt Bf109s, and shot them down, killing one of the pilots, Pilot Officer M. L. Hulton-Harrop. This series of events became known as 'The Battle of Barking Creek', and led to a sweeping review of Fighter Command's plotting systems and operational procedures.

Resulting from the review was the hurried introduction of an Identification Friend or Foe

(IFF) system that was fitted in RAF aircraft thus enabling radar operators to differentiate between enemy and friendly aircraft from their radar signal returns. Initially, the system relied on the 'passive' reflection of radar signals by target aircraft, but an 'active' system that utilised a transponder mounted in the aircraft was in development in early 1939. The principle remains in use today, in both military and civil aviation, albeit in a more sophisticated and reliable form.

Later in September, a Dornier Do.18 flying boat became the first enemy aircraft to be shot down during operations against Britain, the success being credited to a Blackburn Skua of No. 803 Squadron Fleet Air Arm, from H.M.S. Ark Royal. The first Royal Air Force victory, and the first by an aircraft operating from a British land base, took place on October 8 1939. An American-built

Lockheed Hudson of No. 224 Squadron, based at RAF Leuchars, shot down another Dornier Do.18 flying boat to achieve this milestone victory.

Britain's flying boats were generally used for long-range anti-submarine and shipping patrols. Developed from the Short Brothers range of civil aircraft, the Sunderland was a particularly useful aircraft in this role. With an endurance of around 20 hours, the Sunderland was a significant improvement on the earlier biplane flying boats; with self-defence armament that earned it the German nickname of 'flying porcupine', it frequently beat-off attacks by numbers of enemy aircraft, including one occasion when it shot down three out of a group of six Junkers Ju 88s, and caused the three remaining to disengage.

MAIN
Sunderland flying boat at anchor, 1940.

Although the Sunderland was a true 'boat', in that it required a beaching trolley to move it onto dry land, the American-built Consolidated Catalina was an amphibian, with retractable wing tip floats and undercarriage. The Catalina was a classic aircraft of its time: more than 600 were acquired by the RAF, and served with distinction throughout World War II.

The Battle of Britain

Following the resignation of the Prime Minister, Neville Chamberlain in May 1940, the appointment of his successor, Winston Churchill, seemed to give Britain a new-found strength against adversity. Churchill was renowned for his rousing, if somewhat theatrical, speeches and the

Royal Air Force, in particular, was on the receiving end of some of his most impassioned oratory. During the summer of 1940, he signalled the effort that was required to massively increase the strength of Bomber Command, with the following words: *"The Navy can lose us the war, but only the Air Force can win it. Therefore our supreme effort must be to gain overwhelming mastery in the air. The Fighters are our salvation, but the Bombers alone provide the means of victory."*

At the start of the war, Germany had around 4,000 aircraft compared to Britain's front-line strength of 1,660. After the fall of France, the Luftwaffe had almost 3,000 aircraft based in the near continent including 1,400 bombers, 300 dive-bombers, 800 single-engine fighters and 240 twin-engine fighter-bombers. The RAF total included around 800 Hurricanes and Spitfires, of which

LEFT
Pilots scramble to their Hurricane fighters in 1939.

BELOW
Boulton Paul Defiant fighter, 1940.

there were around 660 serviceable in mid-1940. Production of new aircraft was rapidly increasing but a major problem was the shortage of trained crews to fly them, not least the skilled fighter pilots necessary for air defence duties. In April 1940, the Empire Air Training Scheme (later renamed the British Commonwealth Air Training Plan) was introduced in order to bolster the number of aircrew.

As a necessary preliminary to the invasion of Britain, code-named Operation Sealion, the Germans needed control of the Channel ports, in order to prevent Royal Navy forces attacking her invasion fleet that was intended to land on the beaches of Kent and Sussex. To gain such control, the Germans also needed to control the air. Although it possessed large numbers of bombers, the Luftwaffe's fighters had insufficient range to give the bombers adequate air cover for much of their time over British territory. With the benefit of radar, and the visual sightings of enemy aircraft by the Observer Corps, from their posts in Kent and around the Thames estuary, fighter controllers were able to plot the positions of enemy aircraft while they were over the south-east corner of England.

The main phase of the battle began on July 10 1940. By the end of that month, RAF losses were around 150 aircraft, while the Luftwaffe had lost almost 270. In August, the Germans began to attack the airfields of Fighter Command, together with its operations rooms and radar stations, in an attempt to destroy the RAF on the ground. The fact that most of the Stuka dive-bombers had already been destroyed by this time had reduced the Luftwaffe's ability to carry out sufficiently accurate bombing attacks on the British radar stations for them to be taken out of operation. A period of bad weather also hampered the German effort. Even so, their attacks on RAF airfields put six of the seven main fighter bases out of action in the two weeks following August 23, including Biggin Hill which was almost totally destroyed. However, German losses were mounting: during this offensive they lost around 1,000 aircraft, while the Royal Air Force lost 550.

Around this time, the Germans made a series of strategic and tactical errors. Goering, the Luftwaffe commander, ordered the bombing of British radar installations to cease. This was due to his mistaken belief that the stations were of little importance. The Germans also turned their bombing attacks toward Britain's cities, in an attempt to demoralise the civilian population into surrender. These changes in policy proved to be decisive factors in the battle.

The last major air engagement in this phase of the war took place on September 15 1940, a date that will be forever remembered by the Royal Air Force as 'Battle of Britain Day'. On that fateful day, 60 Luftwaffe aircraft were destroyed, at the cost to the RAF of 28 of its own. On September 17, Hitler postponed, indefinitely, the invasion of Britain and turned his attentions towards Russia, although his 'Blitzkrieg' bombing attacks against Britain's towns and cities continued. Propaganda claims and counter-claims were rife; at one point the Germans claimed the destruction of over 3,000 RAF aircraft, more than its entire strength, the actual tally being around 650. In turn, the British government claimed that the RAF had shot down 2,698 German aircraft, whereas this figure should have been around 1,100.

After the battle, Winston Churchill made another of his memorable speeches, in which he made the unforgettable statement: *"Never in the field of human conflict was so much owed by so many to so few."*

Bombs Gone!

In the early months of the war, Royal Air Force bombers based in Britain were used mainly against enemy shipping, often in their ports, or at their anchorage off the German coast. In the first major attack on German land targets, on May 10 1940, eight Whitley bombers from Nos. 77 and 102 Squadrons raided communications sites located inland, to the west of the Rhine. The strategic air offensive against targets within Germany began on May 15 1940, when a Bomber Command force of 99 aircraft struck at 16 separate targets in the Ruhr area. Although no aircraft were lost to enemy action, a Vickers Wellington from No. 115

MAIN
The Spitfire and
the Hurricane,
defenders of
the Realm.

Squadron crashed into high ground near Rouen,
in France, killing its crew of five.

Before the retreat from continental Europe,
ten squadrons of Fairey Battle light bombers of the
Advanced Air Striking Force (AASF) operated
there in support of ground troops. On September
20 1940, the first aerial engagement between the
RAF and the Luftwaffe took place near
Saarbrücken, when three Messerschmitt Bf109s
attacked three Fairey Battles of No. 88 Squadron,
AASF. Two of the Battles were shot down.

The first long-range bombing raid of the war
took place on the night of June 11 1940 when a
force of 36 Armstrong Whitworth Whitley aircraft
from Nos. 10, 51, 77, and 102 Squadrons set out
from Britain, for targets in Italy. Stopping to refuel

in the Channel Islands, they were hampered by bad weather. As a consequence, only thirteen made their attacks on the Italian cities of Genoa and Turin. Two aircraft failed to return. Three days later, aircraft from the Bomber Command unit known as 'Haddock Force', based in the south of France, mounted their first operation against an Italian target as Vickers Wellingtons of Nos. 99 and 149 Squadrons took off from Salon. However, due to particularly bad weather, only one aircraft was able to attack the target at Genoa. The Haddock Force was disbanded shortly afterwards, mainly because of objections from the local government, who ordered the blocking of runways, by French soldiers. This was to prevent the bombers from taking off on missions that, the locals believed, would lead to reprisals against the local population by the German forces.

During the period of the Battle of Britain, the RAF continued to carry out bombing raids over enemy occupied territories. Blenheim bombers frequently targeted the German invasion fleet that

was gathering in the Channel ports of France. These aircraft were also used against military installations and airfields in Norway, and strategic targets in Germany, including the Dortmund-Ems canal. The 'intruder' attacks against airfields were carried out in daylight, and resulted in heavy losses of valuable aircraft and crews. One such attack on July 9 1940, against the Norwegian airfield at Stavanger, resulted in the loss of seven of the twelve aircraft involved. A day later, No. 107 Squadron lost five out of the six Blenheims that raided the French city of Amiens.

Strategic targets in Germany received the attention of Bomber Command throughout the war. In particular, the canals and waterways of the German transport system were bombed on a regular basis, especially their lock gates, bridges and aqueducts. The main targets were the Dortmund-Ems and Mittelland Canals, and the Munster Aqueduct, which were heavily defended by anti-aircraft batteries, resulting in heavy losses of RAF aircraft. Until late September 1940, relatively small numbers of Hampden bombers,

RIGHT
September 1940: A Fairey Battle light-bomber being loaded with 250-pound general purpose bombs.

BELOW
Ground crew reloading a Hurricane fighter's machine guns during the Battle of Britain.

usually groups of less than 20 aircraft, carried out the raids. There followed a lull in the attacks until September 1943, when they were resumed, now by Lancasters and Mosquitoes, and continued until March 1945. Much larger numbers of bombers, sometimes over 200, carried out these raids, with their targets being identified and marked by the Mosquitoes of the Pathfinder force. The raids culminated in the destruction of the Bielefeld Viaduct, on March 14 1945, when a Lancaster of No. 617 Squadron dropped a 22,000lb bomb, the 'Grand Slam', with devastating effect.

After the war, Albert Speer, in his book 'Inside the Third Reich' wrote that... *"of all the strategic attacks made on Germany, the raids on the canals had by far the greatest effect on the German war effort."*

The Thousand Bomber Raids

A series of 'thousand bomber' raids took place between the end of May and mid-August 1942. The idea of Sir Arthur Harris, the C-in-C of Bomber Command, the policy was designed to both destroy enemy targets and enhance the status of his command, which was under threat from political sources. The principle was controversial then, as it would be now: the concept of attempting to force the enemy into submission by attacking largely civilian targets was not popular

ABOVE
June 20 1945: The Handley-Page Halifax III bomber 'Friday the 13th' on exhibition at the site of Lewis's bombed store in Oxford Street, London. The miniature bombs denote 118 of the 128 missions completed. The medal ribbons represent the VC, DSO and DFC decorations won by its crews. The slogan reads 'As Ye Sow, So Shall Ye Reap'.

among his contemporaries. However, having
convinced both Churchill and the Chief of Air
Staff Sir Charles Portal, himself previously head of
Bomber Command, Harris proceeded to assemble
sufficient numbers of aircraft for the raids. Using
an eclectic assortment of aircraft and crews,
including instructors, and crews that were in the
later stages of their training, Harris achieved the
total number that was required. This was in spite
of the withdrawal of some 250 Coastal Command
aircraft, which were initially offered by its C-in-C,
Sir Philip Joubert, then rescinded, under pressure
from the Admiralty Board, who were trying to
maintain control of maritime aircraft for their own
operations. Even so, as many as 49 aircraft, out of
the 208 provided by 91 Group, Bomber
Command, were being flown by trainee pilots.
The number of aircraft being flown by these
novice crews contributed in no small way to the
total of 1,047 bombers taking part. The first raid
was planned to be against Hamburg but, due to
bad visibility over the target, it was Cologne that

received the attentions of the British bombers.
Major damage to factories, infrastructure and
housing ensued, resulting in a quarter of the
population fleeing the city. Bomber Command
lost 41 aircraft on that one night.

The 1,000-bomber raids were mainly
successful. Losses through collision between the
close formation aircraft were relatively few, the
effect on the morale of Bomber Command
personnel improved, as its future was assured, and
the effect on the enemy was devastating. The raids
also served to elevate the stature of 'Bomber'
Harris in the public eye. Although the raids were
restricted mainly to targets nearer the coast during
the short summer nights, other targets still received
visits from Lancasters and other British aircraft.
Not all were successful in their missions, notably
those carrying out attacks against Essen and
Duisburg. However, the bomber raids over
Germany, in which large numbers of aircraft were
used, continued. On June 21 1943, a total of 705
bombers attacked Krefeld, and virtually destroyed
the city. Of that number, 44 aircraft were lost,

mainly to attack by night fighters. At the end of July and beginning of August, further large-scale raids took place on Hamburg, by 777 aircraft, and Nuremburg by 740 aircraft. These totals include aircraft from both Bomber Command and the American 8th Army Air Force, who took part in large numbers with their B-17 Flying Fortress aircraft.

The Dambusters

Formed on March 21 1943, under the command of Wing Commander Guy Gibson, No. 617 Squadron was staffed by crews specially selected for the particular nature of the missions it was to undertake. Their targets were to be the Mohne and Eder Dams, in the Ruhr valley. After six weeks intensive training a total of 19 Lancasters was dispatched in three waves, each aircraft armed with a 'bouncing' bomb, developed by Barnes Wallis, for the specific purpose of attacking, and destroying, these German dams. The entire operation was to be carried out at low level, to escape attack from German night fighters, and the bombs were to be released at a specific height, just above surface of the water behind the dams.

Only twelve of the Lancasters made it to the target area. Wing Commander Gibson's aircraft and four others bombed the Mohne Dam, and breached it, in spite of intense fire from the defending flak guns. Three aircraft went on to breach the Eder Dam, while two others unsuccessfully attacked the Sorpe Dam, as did a single aircraft against the Schwelme Dam. The twelfth aircraft failed to find

its target. Three aircraft were shot down after they had completed their bombing run. For this raid, which caused widespread damage and flooding in the Ruhr valley, and also for a series of other exceptionally courageous missions, Gibson was later awarded the Victoria Cross. Of his comrades, 34 received decorations.

Peenemunde

A major bomber offensive, code-named Operation Hydra, on the night of August 17/18 1943 involved a total of 596 aircraft from Bomber Command. Their target, Peenemunde, was the main experimental establishment where the V-1 flying bomb and the V-2 rocket were developed and tested. A diversionary raid on Berlin, code named Operation Whitebait, was made by a force of Mosquitos. The main stream of bombers en route to Peenemunde met with little opposition from night fighters. The reason given at the time was that the raid on Peenemunde was made on a reciprocal heading from that expected by the

MAIN
Avro Lancaster of
the Battle of Britain
Memorial Flight.

Germans, the initial course of the bomber stream being in a direction that indicated a possible attack in the area of Berlin. This belief was made credible by the diversionary raid carried out by the Mosquitoes. After overflying the Jutland peninsula, the bombers then turned to make their bombing runs from a south-easterly direction. In a raid that was the largest carried out by Bomber Command in the second half of the war, against such a small objective, it was also the first in which a 'Master Bomber' had directed operations over the target. The attack was considered successful in that it delayed the development of the V-2 by several months, thereby reducing the overall effectiveness of the German rocket attacks. Unfortunately, the attack also resulted in the deaths of several hundred foreign workers, mostly of Polish origin, as some bombs fell on a workers camp. Bomber Command lost 23 Lancasters, 15 Halifaxes, and 2 Stirlings, most of these falling victim to the late-arriving Messerschmitt Me-110 night fighters. Two of the fighters, equipped with twin 'Schrage Musik' upward firing 20mm cannon armament, shot down at least six of the bombers as they attacked the homeward-bound aircraft stream.

Dresden, February 1945

One of the most controversial, as well as being one of the most devastating, attacks carried out on a single target was the bombing of Dresden, in February 1945. This raid was part of the Combined Bomber Offensive, in which night attacks were carried out by the RAF, followed the next day with raids by bombers of the 8th United States Army Air Force (USAAF). The political

LEFT
Bristol Beaufort,
circa 1943.

justification for this offensive was to assist the Russian advance from the east and, at the same time, achieve military aims, including those of hindering the German's communications and troop movements. The intention was to create firestorms by dropping large quantities of incendiary bombs over a specific target, thus causing the extremely hot air to rise rapidly, and also draw colder air rapidly towards the centre of the conflagration. The intense heat and strong winds would cause considerable damage to both life and property in the target area. Dresden was considered to be a good target, being relatively lightly defended by anti-aircraft batteries. Alternative targets were designated at Chemnitz and Leipzig: all were located behind the German front, close to the line of battle as the Russians advanced westward, and all were major communications centres crucial to the German war plan.

On February 13 1945, the RAF sent 773 Lancasters to bomb Dresden. This was followed up over the next two days by more than five hundred bombers from the USAAF, resulting in the near-destruction of a city with a population of more than 650,000, and causing many thousands of refugees to flee the Russian advance.

As the war drew towards its inevitable end, there was a more humanitarian motive to the flights carried out by some aircraft of Bomber Command. In Operation Manna, RAF bombers took part in mass food drops to the Dutch population, in areas that were still occupied by German forces. Between April 29 and May 8 1945, approximately 6,685 tons of food were delivered by the RAF, together with a further 3,700 tons dropped by the 8th USAAF.

First Jet Operations

The first operational jet fighter squadron in the Royal Air Force was No. 616 Squadron, a detached flight of seven Meteor F.Mk I aircraft being established at RAF Manston, in Kent, in July 1944. Because of their greater speed, these aircraft were used to chase and destroy V-1 flying bombs, by shooting them down over the sea or open countryside, before they could reach their targets farther inland. One famous event took place in August 1944 when, after all four of his guns had jammed, Flying Officer Dean manoeuvred his aircraft alongside the V-1, and used the disturbed airflow from his wing-tip to tip the flying bomb over, causing it to crash. This was the first destruction of a V-1 by a jet fighter; the squadron also destroyed a second flying bomb on the same day.

The improved Meteor III joined the squadron in December 1944 and, in January 1945, a detached flight from No. 616 Squadron was moved to Belgium. In the following April, the squadron took part in the first offensive operation by RAF jet aircraft when they attacked the Luftwaffe airfield at Nordholz.

Heroic Deeds

During World War II, there were many acts of great heroism carried out in the air by those on active duty with the Royal Air Force. Not all were British: many airmen from the Commonwealth, while serving with the RAF, were decorated for acts of unimaginable courage and bravery in the face of enemy action, or in its aftermath. Many paid the ultimate price, and their honours were awarded posthumously. In their memory, and in recognition of all those who were awarded Britain's highest military honour, the following citation is reproduced here:

Extract from The London Gazette, October 11 1946:

The KING has been graciously pleased to confer the VICTORIA CROSS on the undermentioned officer in recognition of most conspicuous bravery:- Pilot Officer Andrew Charles Mynarski (Can./J.87544) (deceased), Royal Canadian Air Force, No. 419 (R.C.A.F.) Squadron.

Pilot Officer Mynarski was the mid-upper gunner of a Lancaster aircraft, detailed to attack a target at Cambrai in France, on the night of 12th June, 1944. The aircraft was attacked from below and astern by an enemy fighter and ultimately came down in flames.

As an immediate result of the attack, both port engines failed. Fire broke out between the mid-upper turret and the rear turret, as well as in the port wing. The flames soon became fierce and the captain ordered the crew to abandon the aircraft.

Pilot Officer Mynarski left his turret and went towards the escape hatch. He then saw that the rear gunner was still in his turret and apparently unable to leave it. The turret was, in fact, immovable, since the hydraulic gear had been put out of action when the port engines failed, and the manual gear had been broken by the gunner in his attempts to escape.

Without hesitation, Pilot Officer Mynarski made his way through the flames in an endeavour to reach the rear turret and release the gunner. Whilst so doing, his parachute and his clothing up to the waist were set on fire. All his efforts to move the turret and free the rear gunner were in vain. Eventually the rear gunner clearly indicated to him that there was nothing more he could do and that he should try to save his own life. Pilot Officer Mynarski reluctantly went back through the flames to the escape

MAIN
Meteor F Mk.III of No. 616 Squadron, in Belgium, 1945.

hatch. There, as a last gesture to the trapped gunner, he turned towards him, stood to attention in his flaming clothing, and saluted, before he jumped out of the aircraft. Pilot Officer Mynarski's descent was seen by French people on the ground. Both his parachute and his clothing were on fire. He was found eventually by the French, but was so severely burnt that he died from his injuries.

The rear gunner had a miraculous escape when the aircraft crashed. He subsequently testified that had Pilot Officer Mynarski not attempted to save his comrade's life, he could have left the aircraft in safety and would, doubtless, have escaped death.

Pilot Officer Mynarski must have been fully aware that in trying to free the rear gunner he was almost certain to lose his own life. Despite this, with outstanding courage and complete disregard for his own safety, he went to the rescue. Willingly accepting the danger, Pilot Officer Mynarski lost his life by a most conspicuous act of heroism which called for valour of the highest order.

During the course of the war, Royal Air Force personnel took part in operations in many parts of the world, often in conditions of great hardship. Ranging from Europe, to the deserts of North Africa and the jungles of the Far East, the RAF played a vital part in the ultimate victory. The prophecy of Churchill, made in the dark days of 1940, was fulfilled. "…The Fighters are our salvation, but the Bombers alone provide the means of victory."

Chapter Six

A New Dawn

After the end of the war in Europe, the Royal Air Force operated within Germany to assist the British Army in maintaining order within the British Zone of occupation, and was initially tasked with supervising the dissolution of the Luftwaffe. Under the command of Air Chief Marshal Sir William Sholto Douglas, the RAF Second Tactical Air Force (2TAF) was re-designated British Air Forces of Occupation (BAFO). This designation remained until 1951, when the title reverted to its original form, and became fondly known, by some RAF personnel, as 'Second TAF' or, 'Two TAF'.

In the Far East area of operations, the ending of the war against Japan did not result in a peaceful time for the RAF. In September 1945, the RAF South East Asia Command established an Air Headquarters in the Dutch East Indies to oversee the RAF involvement in the repatriation of Allied internees. No. 28 Squadron, with its Spitfire FR XIV aircraft, arrived in Medan to ensure the Nationalist forces of the newly declared Republic of Indonesia did not disrupt the process. These Spitfires were joined by a flight of Mosquito FB VI aircraft from No. 110 Squadron in Batavia, and 'A' Flight of No. 656 Squadron with their Auster AOP V reconnaissance aircraft, at Surabaya, during the same month. RAF involvement in the Dutch East Indies continued until the end of 1946, when it was gradually wound down before eventually ceasing, at the end of November, having flown 19,533 sorties in that campaign.

Trouble was also brewing in French Indo-China, the present-day Vietnam. Following its deployment to Tan Son Nhut airfield at Saigon, No. 273 Squadron flew armed sorties in their Spitfire IX aircraft in support of British troops in the French colony. They were joined at their new base by a flight of Mosquito PR 34 aircraft from No. 684 Squadron that were engaged on photomapping duties. Douglas Dakota transports

of No. 267 squadron also operated from the Tan Son Nhut base, together with a unit of Japanese transport aircraft that were flown by Japanese crews under British command, designated Gremlin Force, in support of British and French ground forces. The Gremlin Force flew over 2,000 sorties before being disbanded in January 1946, along with No. 273 Squadron, while No. 267 Squadron returned to their base in Burma.

Post-war re-organisation

Many changes took place within the Royal Air Force following the cessation of hostilities in World War II. On January 1 1946, Air Chief Marshal Sir Sholto Douglas was promoted to Marshal of the Royal Air Force, and Marshal of the Royal Air Force Sir Arthur Tedder was created Baron, and succeeded Lord Portal as Chief of the Air Staff. During 1946, RAF Reserve Command was formed, the Empire Central Flying School was renamed the Empire Flying School, and the Central Flying school was re-formed at RAF Little Rissington. It was also announced that the Auxiliary Air Force was to be re-established, and would be organised into 13 day-fighter, 3 night-fighter, and 4 light-bomber squadrons. The Air Ministry also decided that the Royal Air Force Regiment would continue as an organic part of the RAF, and would comprise a number of rifle, armoured car, and light anti-aircraft (LAA) squadrons. Some units of the RAF Regiment would also become parachute capable.

As the service was scaled down from its wartime status, it was reduced in manpower from

LEFT
RAF truck overturned
and set alight during
disturbances in
Allenby Road, Tel
Aviv, August 1947.

BELOW
Living quarters at
RAF Station El
Firdan, Egypt, 1953.

1,100,000 to around 358,000 by the end of June 1946. Responsibility for the control of overseas-based transport aircraft resources was to be transferred from Transport Command to the relevant overseas command, except for the strategic 'route' supply and trooping services from the UK, that were to remain with Transport Command.

The new year, 1947, began with an agreement to establish exchange postings between the Royal Air Force and the United States Army Air Force. It was not long before the RAF was, once again, in action in the Middle East. This time it was the Aden Protectorate that was the focus of attention. In February, after local unrest, a fort occupied by dissidents was attacked by a force of RAF Regiment armoured cars, in support of ground troops belonging to the Aden Protectorate Levies. Mosquitoes of No. 8 Squadron gave aerial support, in the form of rocket attacks. Further skirmishes took place on several occasions during the year and culminated in the almost total destruction of the village of Thumier in October 1947. In an effort to avoid civilian casualties a leaflet drop, giving warning of impending action, preceded the attack. No. 8 Squadron, by now equipped with Hawker Tempest ground attack aircraft, and supported by Lincoln bombers from No. 101 Squadron, carried

out the raid. The actions by dissidents continued, at intervals, throughout the next twenty years, leading to the eventual withdrawal of all British forces from Aden, by 1967.

Palestine

The Royal Air Force in the Middle East suffered the total loss of some of its aircraft, and damage to others, in a series of terrorist attacks on bases in Palestine during February 1947. In one of these attacks, seven Spitfires, 11 Halifaxes, and two Ansons were destroyed, or damaged beyond economical repair, on one single night. There were also frequent attacks on British military patrols and transport outside the bases, causing damage to vehicles and disruption to British Army and RAF movements.

In a rapidly deteriorating situation, Operation Polly was initiated in order to evacuate all non-essential civilians. In two days, Halifax transport aircraft from No. 113 Squadron evacuated 508 persons to Egypt. Following the partitioning of the former Palestine, and the establishment of the new state of Israel, the RAF began the withdrawal from their bases in the area. During the latter stages of the withdrawal, the Egyptian Air force carried out three separate attacks, in error, on the RAF airfield

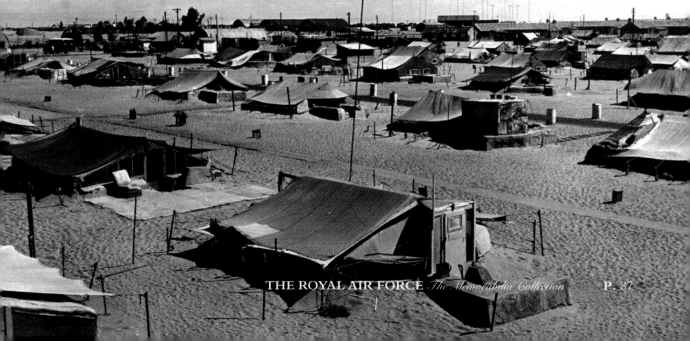

at Ramat David. During these attacks, ten Spitfires from Nos. 32 and 208 Squadrons were damaged, two being totally destroyed. A Dakota from No. 204 Squadron was also destroyed, and a further two damaged, as were three Austers. Four of the attackers were shot down by RAF Spitfires, and a fifth by anti-aircraft fire.

Malaya

The month of June 1948 heralded trouble on two fronts for Britain's forces. In the Federation of Malaya, following rioting and civil unrest, the High Commissioner, Sir Edward Gent, declared a state of emergency. The Malayan Communist Party was banned a month later, effectively marking the beginning of Operation Firedog. During the Malaya Emergency, a total of 15 RAF squadrons were involved in the campaign, with many UK-based units being temporarily detached to the area. On July 6 1948, the Royal Air Force flew its first offensive mission of Operation

Firedog, when Spitfires of No. 60 Squadron attacked, and destroyed, a communist terrorist camp in Perak. This was the first of many counter-terrorist operations in a campaign that was to continue until 1960.

Berlin Airlift

The second major involvement for the Royal Air Force was somewhat closer to home. The Soviets initiated a military blockade on all land and water routes through the Russian Zone of Germany, effectively isolating the western-controlled sector of Berlin. This left only three, 20 mile-wide air corridors, over Russian territory,

MAIN
Handley Page
Hastings being
unloaded in the
British Sector of
Berlin, 1949.

which could be used to supply the inhabitants. The allies were faced with the stark choice between allowing the inhabitants of Berlin to starve, or attempting to supply their basic necessities for life, by air. In choosing the latter, they were faced with a mammoth task. The first day of Operation Vittles, the American part of the airlift, began on June 26 1948 when United States Air Force (USAF) Dakotas delivered a meagre 80 tons of food to the beleaguered city. This was only a fraction of the estimated daily requirement for 4,500 tons of food, coal, and other necessary goods, to ensure the survival of the 2.5 million inhabitants. It was not known at the time that this effort would need to be sustained for a period of eleven months.

Two days later, RAF Dakota transport aircraft of No. 46 Group began to supply the British

military garrison in Berlin, in Operation Knicker. On the following day, June 29, supplies for the civilian population began to be delivered in Operation Carter Patterson, a name the Russians knew well, as it belonged to a British removals company of that time. To dispel any thoughts the Russians may have had about the possibility of a withdrawal by Britain, on July 3 the name was changed to Operation Plainfare, a play on words that was particularly appropriate. On the same day, RAF Avro York transport aircraft flew their first missions into Berlin. Two days later, they were joined in the airlift by Sunderland flying boats of Nos. 201 and 230 Squadrons, Coastal Command, flying between Hamburg and the Haval See, a large lake situated within the boundaries of Berlin.

The Soviets did their best to disrupt the airlift. In spite of being harassed by Russian fighters, barrage balloons being set loose across the air lanes, and the jamming of radio signals, the airlift was successful in more than just its primary objective. One of the lessons learned by the Allies in the co-ordination and close control of air traffic led to the subsequent establishment of the civil 'airways' corridor system that is now used throughout the world. Also, the standardisation of aircraft loading and unloading procedures, and other benefits resulting from mutual operations, could be put into use in later humanitarian relief scenarios. The airlift also highlighted the need for dedicated cargo aircraft to be built for both military, and civilian, purposes; this resulted in the development, by the Americans, of the C-130, C-141 and C-5 aircraft types.

At times, aircraft were landing in Berlin at a rate of one every three minutes, and during the airlift, a total of 2.3 million tons, from 277, 569 flights, was delivered. The RAF delivered 281,727 short tons of freight into Berlin, flew 29,532 short tons out to the West, and carried 67,373 passengers. The Lancastrian, York, and Hastings transport aircraft, and the Sunderlands of Coastal Command, altogether flew 18,205,284 miles during 49,733 sorties. Although the Russians lifted the blockade on May 12 1949, the airlift continued until September of that year in order to create a stockpile of supplies.

Korea

Following the outbreak of the Korean War in 1950, No. 88 Squadron commenced maritime reconnaissance operations with their Sunderland flying boats from Iwakuni, Japan, in support of the United Nations blockade of North Korea. Further Sunderland operations were carried out, on

RIGHT
Pilot of No. 8 Squadron pictured in his Vampire fighter in Kenya, 1954.

BELOW
Vampire and Meteor aircraft undergoing maintenance in the Canal Zone of Egypt, in 1956.

were awarded the Distinguished Flying Cross, six were Mentioned in Dispatches, and four were decorated with Air Medals by the United States.

Elsewhere in the Korean War, 21 Royal Air Force pilots served on attachment with either the 4th, or the 51st, Fighter Interceptor Wings of the USAF. Of these, four failed to return from operational sorties, including Wing Commander J.R. Baldwin, a veteran of World War II fighter operations, who was declared missing in action on March 15 1952. Each of the RAF pilots damaged one or more North Korean Mikoyan-Gurevich MiG15s in combat. One pilot, Squadron Leader G.S. Hulse, was credited with achieving two kills before failing to return from a sortie on March 13 1953; a further 5 were credited with one kill each.

The RAF in Britain's Little Wars

The formal state of war between Britain and Germany ended officially on July 9 1951. Since then, the RAF has continued to be involved in airlifting troops and supplies, in support of British, Allied, and Commonwealth forces, in a series of operations around the world that have continued, sporadically, into the 21st Century. Several times in the 1950s, the RAF was called upon to deliver troops and equipment to trouble spots in Egypt and East Africa. In October 1951, after fighting broke out around the British bases in the Canal Zone, the 16th Independent Parachute Brigade was flown from Cyprus in Vickers Vikings of Nos. 70, 78, 114, 204 and 216 Squadrons, to reinforce units stationed in the Canal Zone.

On October 9 1952, a State of Emergency was declared in Kenya. On that day, Hastings transport aircraft of No. 511 Squadron carried men from the Lancashire Fusiliers into Nairobi, to reinforce British Army units and Kenyan forces operating against Mau Mau terrorists. RAF aircraft took part in many operations against Mau Mau terrorists, including sorties by Harvards of No. 1340 Flight,

monthly rotation, with the addition of Nos. 205 and 209 Squadrons, until July 31 1953. Hastings transport aircraft from No. 53 Squadron began casualty evacuation flights between Iwakuni and the UK in September 1950. Although no Royal Air Force combat aircraft were involved in the Korean conflict, a total of 32 RAF pilots took part when they were attached to No. 77 Squadron, Royal Australian Air Force (RAAF). Officially, they were on secondment to help convert Australian pilots onto the ex-RAF Meteor F8 fighters that had been acquired by the RAAF. Of the RAF pilots, four were killed in action, one was killed in a flying accident, and one, Flying Officer M.O.Berg, became a prisoner of war when forced to eject from his Gloster Meteor F8, after it had been damaged by anti-aircraft fire. Four RAF pilots

Rock Apes and Rifles

The Royal Air Force Regiment is a specialist Branch within the Royal Air Force, responsible for defending airfields and associated installations. Members of the Regiment are 'affectionately' known within the RAF as 'Rock Apes' or 'Rocks' and the organisation itself is simply known as 'The Regiment'. Although it is believed, by some, that the nickname 'Rock Ape' referred to the regiment's association with Gibraltar (The Rock), there is a more colourful version of its origin.

In November 1952, two RAF Regiment officers, serving with the Aden Protectorate Levy (APL) at Dhala, in Western Aden, decided to amuse themselves by going out to shoot some of the baboons that were locally referred to as 'rock apes'. Each armed with a rifle, they separated to hunt the apes. In failing light, one of the officers fired at a distant moving object. When he reached the target, he discovered he had shot his fellow officer. The victim, Flight Lieutenant Mason, survived after receiving emergency treatment, and returned to duty a few months later. When asked by a member of the 'inevitable' Board of Inquiry as to the reason he had fired at his comrade, the officer replied that his target had '…looked just like a rock ape' in the half-light. This remark took little time to circulate around the RAF, and the term 'rock ape' was soon in general use throughout the service.

MAIN
HM Queen Elizabeth II inspects the static display of over 300 aircraft at her Coronation Review, 1953. In the Foreground are Vampires, Sabres, and B-29 bombers that were designated Washington B1 in RAF service.

and Lincoln bombers that 'pattern bombed' the terrorist camps and operating areas.

Notable Events

Changes in organisation, within the service in the late 1940s and 1950s, included the formation of The Women's Royal Air Force (WRAF) on February 1 1949, which replaced the Women's Auxiliary Air Force (WAAF). Later that year, on June 1, the Far East Air Force (FEAF) was formed, and RAF Mediterranean/Middle East was renamed Middle East Air Force (MEAF).

Female emancipation within the RAF was demonstrated when, on September 20 1952, Pilot Officer Jean Lennox Bird, of the Women's Royal Air Force (WRAF) Volunteer Reserve, became the first woman to be awarded Royal Air Force pilot's wings. Another RAF 'first' occurred, also in 1952, when Flight Lieutenant D. Kerns became the first pilot to carry out an air-sea rescue by helicopter, within the UK, when he rescued four Danish seamen off the coast of Yarmouth.

A momentous event, The Coronation Review of the Royal Air Force, took place at RAF Odiham, Hampshire, in July 1953. HM Queen Elizabeth II carried out a review of 300 static aircraft, their crews, and ground support personnel. The highlight of the day's events was a fly past of 640 aircraft, including 440 jet-engine aircraft.

Having previously carried out similar sorties, some two years earlier, three North American RB45C Tornado aircraft belonging to the USAF, but bearing RAF markings and flown by RAF crews, flew reconnaissance sorties over the Soviet Union from the USAF base at RAF Sculthorpe, in April 1953. All returned safely to base, although one aircraft had been engaged by anti-aircraft artillery.

A chapter in the history of the Royal Air Force came to an end, on February 10 1956, with the death of Marshal of the Royal Air Force Viscount Hugh Montague Trenchard of Wolfeton, at his home in London, aged 83. The great man, known as 'Boom Trenchard' because of his loud speaking voice, and often referred to as 'The Father of the Royal Air Force', is buried in the Battle of Britain Chapel, at Westminster Abbey.

The first Avro Vulcan B1 bomber to be taken on charge by the RAF, XA 897, was lost in a crash while on approach to land at London Heathrow airport in poor weather, on September 9 1956. This aircraft was returning from Operation Tasman Flight, a flag-waving tour of Australia and New Zealand. The pilot and co-pilot ejected, successfully, but the four-man rear crew, none of whom were provided with ejection seats, all lost their lives. The lack of ejection facilities for rear-seated crew in all three types of Britain's V-bombers, and in some marks of the Canberra, was the subject of much debate, both within the RAF, and elsewhere.

Trouble flared, again, in the Middle East, towards the end of 1956. Israel had attacked bases within Sinai, in Egypt, from which Egyptian forces had raided Israel. Following an ultimatum issued

BELOW
The ill-fated Bristol Brigand seen here in 1946. After entering service with the RAF in Malaya in 1949, this type was subsequently grounded following a series of accidents.

by Britain and France to the two adversaries, which was accepted by Israel but rejected by Egypt, the RAF once more took to the skies in the Middle East. Canberra and Valiant bombers carried out bombing raids on twelve Egyptian airfields in the Nile Delta and the Canal Zone. This series of raids included the first operational use of a V-bomber, albeit in a conventional role, and successfully neutralised the Egyptian Air Force while it was on the ground. RAF aircraft continued operations in support of ground troops and, together with aircraft of both the French Air Force and their naval comrades Aeronavale, carried out further attacks on targets in preparation for an amphibious assault on Port Said in November. In December, a United Nations peacekeeping force

took over in the Canal Zone, prior to the withdrawal of British and French forces.

The predecessor of the Battle of Britain Memorial Flight (BBMF) was formed at RAF Biggin Hill, Kent, in July 1957. The Historic Aircraft Flight, as it was then known, received three Spitfire PR Mk XIX aircraft, in addition to its Hurricane LF363.

In April 1958 the two-man crew of a Canberra bomber made an unscheduled entry into the record books when they were forced to eject at an altitude of almost 57,000 feet. Both survived their ordeal. Later that year, on October 19, the Church of the Royal Air Force, St. Clement Danes on the Strand, London was re-consecrated, in the presence of the Queen. The church had been heavily damaged during bombing in 1941 and had been partially restored prior to it being dedicated to the RAF.

January 1 1959 heralded another eventful year for the post-war RAF, in which the Royal Air Force's 2nd Tactical Air Force was renamed Royal Air Force Germany, RAF Home Command was disbanded, and Marshal of the Royal Air Force Sir William Dickson became the first Chief of the Defence Staff. The end of the Fifties decade also marked the end of the flying boat in RAF service, the final sorties being flown by two Short Sunderlands of No. 205 Squadron, RAF Seletar, Singapore.

Something Old, Something New, Something Borrowed

The years following the end of World War II saw a variety of aircraft types enter into service with the RAF. Of these, some were later versions of aircraft that had seen wartime service, others were developments or adaptations of existing designs; a comparatively small number were completely new designs.

The Spitfire Mk.21 entered service in 1945, as did the Hawker Tempest II and the Sikorski

Hoverfly, the first helicopter to be operated by the RAF. The latest version of the comparatively new jet fighter, the Gloster Meteor III, joined No. 74 Squadron in the forefront of Britain's air defence duties. Two developments of the Lancaster bomber, the Avro Lincoln bomber, and the Lancastrian transport, were also added to the inventory of RAF aircraft.

In January 1947, one of the more 'shiny' aircraft entered service with the delivery of its first Vickers Viking to The King's Flight at RAF Benson. New fighter aircraft came on stream with the arrival of the first deHavilland Vampire F1 fighters with No. 247 Squadron, which was to be based at RAF Odiham for the next decade. During 1948, No. 47 Squadron became the first RAF transport squadron to receive the Handley Page Hastings C1, just in time to be pressed into service on the Berlin Airlift. This squadron flew over 3,000 sorties in seven months, carrying mainly coal, during the airlift operations. The Gloster Meteor T7 also joined up in 1948, for the start of its lengthy service career. Initially with No. 203 Advanced Flying School, the Meteor T7

served with a great number of RAF units, as testified by the total of 642 of the type that were ordered by the Ministry of Supply, and a further 40 by overseas customers.

In 1949, the Bristol Brigand first appeared in RAF service with No. 84 Squadron, and was involved in counter-terrorist strikes against insurgents during Operation Firedog in Malaya. However, due to a number of accidents, the Brigand was grounded, and withdrawn from service. The same year saw the entry into RAF service of yet another stalwart, the deHavilland Devon, with No. 31 Squadron on communications duties at RAF Hendon. One of this type, Devon C2 serial number VP952, has a claim to being the aircraft with the longest RAF service: having been first delivered in 1949, it flew its last operational flight with No. 207 Squadron on June 29 1984, and is now preserved at the RAF Cosford museum. The Vickers Valetta outlasted its stable-mate, the Viking of The King's Flight, in service as a workhorse with transport squadrons both at home and overseas.

MAIN
Shackleton MR2
on a practice
Search and Rescue
(SAR) mission.

NEXT PAGE
English Electric
Canberra B2.
Britain's first
jet bomber.

The decade of the 1950s saw the entry into service of another great aircraft, favourite of many RAF pilots, the deHavilland Chipmunk two-seat trainer. The 'Chippy', as it was known, was probably the first aircraft that was flown in by many future RAF pilots. University Air Squadrons, where many pilots learned to fly, on scholarships awarded by the RAF, were among those who used the Chipmunk. It was also used extensively for flying Air Training Corps Cadets on air experience flights, which often resulted in the use of the paper bag that was provided for the aftermath of an 'aerobatics initiation' ceremony! The helicopter inventory saw the introduction of the Westland Dragonfly, a license-built version of the Sikorski S-51, and it was soon put to work in the war against terrorists, in Malaya. The much-improved Meteor F8 and FR 9 variants entered service, from 1950, with Nos. 245 and 208 Squadrons, respectively.

By the end of the 1940s, it was obvious that the aging Lincoln bombers that equipped RAF Bomber Command would need to be replaced by 'stop-gap' aircraft, pending the delivery of new jet powered bombers. The first crews from No. 115 Squadron commenced training on the Boeing B-29, in the USA, in March 1950. The first batch, of a total of 87 of the aircraft, designated 'Washington Mk1' by the RAF, later arrived at RAF Marham, Norfolk, flown by their newly trained crews.

Britain's night fighter capability was entrusted to the Armstrong-Whitworth Meteor NF11s, some of which joined No. 29 Squadron in 1951. Maritime reconnaissance duties were taken over by the Avro Shackleton, with No. 120 Squadron of Coastal Command being the first recipients of that type. The 'Shack' was to remain in service, in several incarnations, for many years to come. To fill the maritime patrol requirement prior to the arrival of the Shackleton, another 'stop-gap' was obtained from the USA, in the guise of the Lockheed Neptune MR Mk1 that was first operated by No. 210 Squadron at St.Eval, Cornwall.

The advent of the English Electric Canberra heralded yet another aircraft type that would give

Chapter Six

valuable, and lengthy, service in the Royal Air
Force. In a number of roles, and in several
variants, the Canberra remained in RAF service
for almost half a century. RAF Germany was the
destination for the first two squadrons of
Canadian-built Sabre fighters, Nos. 3 and 234
Squadrons, who operated from their bases at RAF
Geilenkirchen. In fact, only two squadrons of
Sabres, those of Nos. 66 and 92 Squadrons were
based in the UK. Of a total of 427 Sabre F4s
delivered, the majority served in eleven German-
based RAF squadrons.

The Supermarine Swift fighter aircraft was
ordered as a 'fall-back', in case the Hawker Hunter
project failed. With the benefit of hindsight, it was
the Swift that failed to live up to its publicity.
Except for it breaking the world absolute speed
record over Libya on September 26 1953 with a
speed of 735 miles per hour, beating Neville
Duke's record of 727 mph in a Hunter F3 that
was set only three weeks earlier, the Swift was
generally considered to be less than a success, in
RAF service, as a fighter. It later regained some
respectability as a fighter-reconnaissance aircraft.

In stark contrast with the Swift, the Hawker
Hunter, apart from some teething problems, was a
remarkable asset to the RAF, in both the fighter
and ground-attack roles. This good-looking
aircraft attracted the attention of all those who saw
it, either in flight, or on the ground. Few who
witnessed the event could forget the sight of 22
Hunters in a formation 'loop' at Farnborough in
1958, described in 'Flight' magazine as: "...the most
wonderful mass aerobatic manoeuvre ever witnessed at
Farnborough (or, we are moved to declare, elsewhere)."

The Gloster Javelin assumed the mantle of the
all-weather fighter when it entered service with
No. 46 Squadron in 1956. The middle years of the
decade saw even more newcomers to RAF
service: the Blackburn Beverley and the
deHavilland Comet transport aircraft were at

opposite ends of the aesthetic spectrum but both proved valuable assets in their differing roles. These were augmented in 1959 by the arrival in service of the Bristol Britannia; the first squadron to be so equipped was No. 99 Squadron at RAF Lyneham.

Between 1955 and 1959, the RAF received the aircraft it needed to fulfil its strategic bombing capability as the triumvirate of V-bombers began to enter service. First came the eight Vickers Valiant B1s, early in 1955, which formed No. 138 Squadron at Gaydon. In July 1957, No. 83 Squadron received its first Avro Vulcan B1s, and the Handley Page Victor B1 entered service,

initially with No. 232 Operational Conversion Unit, late in 1957, before the formation of No. 10 Squadron, which received its Victor B1s in early 1958.

The Royal Air Force was now ready for any action that might be necessary if the Cold War situation should deteriorate to such a level that retaliatory strikes would become a reality.

BELOW INSET
Blackburn Beverley towering over a Vickers Valetta on the salt pan dispersal at RAF Khormaksar, Aden, in 1959.

MAIN
Sixteen Hawker
Hunters from No.
111. This squadron
performed a
formation 'loop'
with 22 aircraft at
the Farnborough Air
Show in 1958.

Chapter Seven

White Paper and White Bombers

The Defence White Paper – 1957

The disbanding of the Royal Auxiliary Air Force, in March 1957, was the first in a series of political decisions that had a somewhat demoralising effect on the members of the Royal Air Force.

One of the most far-reaching reviews that British defence forces were ever to be subjected to in peacetime affected all three services, in some way or another, and also had a debilitating effect on Britain's defence industry. The political view of the Conservative government of the day was that, in the future, Britain should place far greater reliance on a strategic nuclear deterrent than on conventional military strength and posturing. Following the Suez crisis in 1956, in which the United States had played little part, Britain could no longer rely on either political or military support from the USA. Also, the fact that the Soviet Union had successfully placed a spacecraft, Sputnik 1, in earth orbit, showed that there had been a considerable leap forward in missile technology that could, potentially, pose a major threat to the West, in any escalation from the Cold War status quo. For these reasons, many politicians were in favour of an independent British nuclear deterrent.

In April 1957, the UK government issued a White Paper on Defence. Introduced by the

BELOW
Aircrew pictured on the Canberra flight line at RAF Bassingbourne, Cambridgeshire, in 1952.

Minister of Defence, Duncan Sandys, this document was to have a far-reaching effect on Britain's defence industry as a whole, and a particular effect on the Royal Air Force. Pertinent to the RAF, its main feature was the premise that all manned aircraft would be replaced by guided missiles, by the year 1970. With this philosophy, most existing aircraft development projects could, therefore, be cancelled, and the defence of Britain would be vested in the deterrent effect of its nuclear weapons.

Among the few people who were to benefit directly from the review, would be those reluctant future conscripts who would not now be required to submit themselves to military discipline by call-up for two years National Service in the armed forces. The White Paper predicted that call-up for National Service would end in 1960, with the last conscripts leaving the armed services in 1962. This planning was based on the United Kingdom armed forces having a total strength of 380,000 regular, adult male, uniformed personnel.

Britain's future principal military tasks were defined as:

(a) "…to provide the minimum forces necessary to defend and preserve order in British colonies and other territories which we have to protect (e.g. the Persian Gulf sheikhdoms, and Malaya)"

(b) "…to play our part in preventing world war … by creating a British element of nuclear deterrent power, and … by contributing sufficient land, air and sea forces to maintain the solidarity of the NATO alliance and the involvement of the Americans in Europe, upon which our whole security depends." (This reference to America is somewhat contradictory to the Government statement implying that Britain could no longer rely on the United States for political or military support).

(c) "…to play a modest part, along with other Commonwealth countries and allies in SEATO (South East Asia Treaty Organisation) and the Baghdad Alliance, in deterring Communist aggression or infiltration and preserving stability in those areas."

The White Paper also made the following observation:

"With regular forces of 380,000 it should be just possible, *with difficulty and not without risk,* to carry out these tasks. A tentative plan for the distribution of such forces is set out in Annexe A." (Annexe A then detailed the reduction in forces, in terms of both manpower and their disposition, for all three services – the proposed strength and composition of the RAF is summarised below).

(1) The RAF to have a personnel strength of 135,000 regular adult males.

MAIN
Vulcan B1 in1952.
The white paint
was intended to
protect the aircraft
and crew from the
flash effects of a
nuclear explosion.

(2) Moderate-sized bomber force to be replaced by ballistic rockets with a stock of British-made nuclear bombs (supplemented by American bombs, the use of which to be subject to US control).

(3) Air Defence of Great Britain to be 280 fighters, versus the 480 in service in 1957, limited to the task of protecting bomber bases, to be largely replaced in due course by guided missiles.

(4) Coastal Command to be reduced in strength from twelve to seven squadrons.

(5) Transport Command to be reduced in strength to a total of seven and a half squadrons, including 16 Britannias and 32 Beverleys.

(6) Tactical Air Force in Germany to reduce in strength from 466 aircraft in 1957, initially to 216, then to be further reduced to 104 by 1961. Some four squadrons of Canberras, for assignment to SACEUR (Supreme Allied Commander Europe) would be based in the UK.

(7) In the Near East, and Middle East, four light-bomber squadrons, one transport squadron, and one photo-reconnaissance squadron to be stationed in Cyprus to support Baghdad alliance, four squadrons at Aden, and one maritime squadron at Malta.

(8) Far East Air Force to go from 134 to 74 aircraft, including one light-bomber squadron, one fighter-bomber squadron, one maritime reconnaissance squadron, one photo-reconnaissance squadron, and three transport squadrons. The fighter squadron in Hong Kong to be withdrawn.

The White Paper also contained the following statement: "This plan assumes that these much reduced forces will be well equipped. In particular, our air defence system, when it is converted to rockets, must be armed with nuclear warheads. For this a second uranium diffusion plant is essential."

Some of the reasoning used in the decision making process leading to the White Paper appears to have been flawed. The cost savings obtained in the resultant withdrawal or reduction in forces, from some overseas commitments are undeniable. However, the unit costs of maintaining such forces would still be substantial, when the relative economies of scale are taken into consideration. The air defence of Britain, including the lynch pin of the nuclear deterrent, the V-bomber force, was also the subject of dubious reasoning on the part of those responsible for the White Paper. Elsewhere in the world, other governments were already investing in advanced defence programs, including those of France, the United States, and the Soviet Union.

Of the few remaining defence projects, the English Electric Lightning fighter, while being supersonic in level flight without using its reheat, coupled with a high rate of climb, was hampered by its relatively short range. This necessitated installation of an in-flight refuelling probe, in order to provide a respectable radius of operation. Pilots who flew the Lightning were generally enthusiastic about the aircraft, notwithstanding its shortcomings in range. Its maintenance crews were less than impressed, largely due to its tightly packed equipment, and their unfamiliarity with a complex aircraft and systems: this was compounded by the lack of foresight by planners in failing to provide the sufficient necessary training facilities and support systems. Within a few years, despite its early difficulties, the Lightning had evolved into a potent defender of Britain's skies. When introduced into the RAF, with a planned service life of ten years, it was seen as being little more than a token gesture as, according to the White Paper of 1957, "…all manned aircraft could be replaced by guided missiles, by the year 1970." The Lightning

continued in service with the Royal Air Force until 1988.

White Bombers and Big Bangs – Operation Grapple and the H-bomb

The Royal Air Force carried out its first trial drop of an atomic weapon in October 1956, at the Maralinga weapons range in South Australia. A Vickers Valiant of No. 49 Squadron, with the airframe number WZ366, released a Blue Danube round, with a yield of between three and four kilotons, from an altitude of 30,000 feet.

Blue Danube was the first operational British nuclear weapon; it also went by a variety of other names, including Smallboy, the Mk.1 Atom Bomb, and OR.1001, a reference to the Operational Requirement that called for such a weapon. It was intended as the primary armament of the V-bomber force, the bomb bays of whose aircraft had been designed specifically to hold the Blue Danube. The Blue Danube weapon was

BELOW
Lightning F1 fighters in formation.

RIGHT
The nuclear signature of a mushroom-shaped cloud ascends above ground-zero after detonation of Britain's first H-bomb near Christmas Island on May 15 1957.

LEFT
RAF Gaydon, Warwickshire in 1956. Chief Technician L. Paddock, the aircraft crew chief, standing beneath the tail of a Vickers Valiant.

BELOW
RAF Fylingdales's early warning radar inside its protective 'Golf Ball'.

declared fit for operations in November 1953. In April 1954, at RAF Wittering, a Vickers Valiant unit with the designation No. 1321 Flight was established to integrate the Blue Danube nuclear weapon into RAF service.

In May 1957, the first of a series of tests known as Operation Grapple took place from Christmas Island, in the Pacific, when a Vickers Valiant, XD818, of No. 49 Squadron, successfully dropped a Yellow Sun thermonuclear weapon with a yield of 100 to 150 kilotons.

Air Defence Missiles

In the White Paper of 1957, the defence of V-bomber bases was to be taken over by guided weapons. In development since 1947, the Bristol Bloodhound began to be deployed operationally. There were shortcomings in its effectiveness, not least being the inadequate range, of around 50 miles, and problems with its pulsed radar system being vulnerable to jamming. Coupled with the fact that Bloodhound was designed to operate from a fixed base, the lack of launch-site flexibility

was also a disadvantage. Although most of the problems were overcome in the Bloodhound Mk2, which deployed in the mid-1960s, it still operated from a fixed base, although its range of operation had increased to around 115 miles. The premise that the defence of V-bomber bases could be carried out solely by using guided missiles was erroneous. This placed even greater reliance on manned RAF fighters, and their supporting air defence and ground-based radar systems, to prevent a potential attacker from entering British airspace. In practical terms, there was little defence against any attack by a strategic missile other than the corresponding 'deterrent' of nuclear retaliation against the aggressor.

Strategic Missiles – The Mighty Thor

The RAF entered the strategic nuclear missile arena in 1958, following an agreement with the United States in which the USA would supply sixty Douglas Thor Intermediate Range Ballistic Missiles (IRBM) and their warheads, to Britain, for a period of five years. The first Royal Air

Chapter Seven

Force Thor-equipped missile squadron, No. 77 (SM) Squadron, Bomber Command, was formed at RAF Feltwell in September 1958, albeit without any missiles at this time, as the squadron prepared for the advent of Thor by developing RAF maintenance and launch procedures. Launching of the missiles was to be controlled by means of a coded authentication command and a 'dual key' missile firing and warhead arming protocol. RAF and USAF officers held the dual keys, jointly. The British key could initiate a launch: however, the USAF key retained the arming of the warhead under United States control. The first launch of a Royal Air Force Thor took place at Vandenberg USAF base, California, by a crew from No. 98 (SM) Squadron, under training.

Blue Steel and Skybolt

It had been recognised, as early as 1954, that because of the medium-range missile defences, it would be dangerous for the proposed V-bombers to over-fly, or approach within 50 miles of, their targets. Therefore, the Ministry of Supply, which was responsible for procurement of defence equipment at that time, placed contracts for the development of a guided bomb that would allow the V-bomber that launched it to 'stand-off' from its target. The bomb was to carry a British nuclear warhead. The fact that no suitable warhead was available for three to five years, coupled with other problems in development, delayed the entry in RAF service of Blue Steel, as it became known, until 1962. The service entry of Blue Steel signalled the end of the Thor IRBM as Britain's nuclear deterrent. A total of around 36 V-bombers were made 'Blue Steel capable', serving until 1969, when Britain's nuclear deterrent was passed to the Royal Navy's Polaris submarine-launched ballistic missile.

In 1959, the USAF awarded a development contract to the Douglas Company for the WS 138A long-range air-launched ballistic missile (ALBM). Subsequently known as the GAM-87 Skybolt, the missile was intended for use by B-52 Stratofortress strategic bombers of the USAF.

RIGHT
Avro Vulcan B2 carrying a Blue Steel stand-off weapon at the Farnborough Air Show in 1958.

BELOW
RAF crew training with a Skybolt missile at USAF base at Eglin, Florida, in 1962.

carried out in great secrecy, and the British government chose not to inform the respective heads of the countries of the events. In a, since declassified, memorandum from 1960, an official in the Air Ministry insisted that all those involved maintain their silence. "All possible measures should be taken in Cyprus to conceal the arrival and storage of nuclear bombs," wrote the official, "whether they be inert or drill or the real McCoy."

By 1960, an area within the RAF base at Akrotiri had been readied for the operational storage of up to 16 Red Beard tactical nuclear weapons. The following year, permanent storage facilities for a further 32 of these weapons was opened nearby at Cape Gata. By the end of 1962, airfield facilities at Akrotiri had been upgraded to handle the Vulcan bombers that had arrived that same year, and were to remain based there, until 1975. Also in 1960, the RAF was making plans for the arrival in Singapore, some two years later, of 48 Red Beard weapons at RAF Tengah. It was originally planned that both the Vulcan and the Canberra would be based at that station, but the Vulcan never became resident other than on a detachment basis, notably during the Indonesian Confrontation of Malaysia when it was intended to be used as a conventional bomber. The Canberra was capable of delivering Red Beard using the LABS (Low Altitude Bombing system) toss-bombing technique, and this remained the primary means of tactical nuclear weapons delivery until around 1970, when the Tengah base was de-activated as an RAF station.

Following the cancellation of the Blue Streak intercontinental ballistic missile program, the British government joined with the Americans in the ALBM project. In RAF service the British Skybolts would be carried by Vulcan B2 aircraft, with the Skybolt supplanting the proposed Blue Steel 2 project, which was then abandoned. Unfortunately for Britain, in 1962, after a series of economic and political problems, the United States cancelled the Skybolt project.

Tactical Nuclear Weapons

As well as being deployed in the UK and Germany, tactical nuclear weapons were deployed as early as 1960, at RAF Akrotiri, on one of Britain's Sovereign Base Areas in southern Cyprus. Two years later Harold Macmillan, then Prime Minister, personally authorised the storage of nuclear weapons at RAF Tengah in Singapore. These activities were

WE177 Nuclear Weapon

The WE177 was destined to be the last air-launched atomic bomb in the inventory of the

United Kingdom. It was a free-fall thermonuclear weapon that became operational in late 1966, replacing Red Beard. It also formed the basis for a nuclear depth charge that was deployed on vessels of the Royal Navy. It was produced in three main variants, with respective yields of 200, 400 and 10 kilotons. The first two variants were intended to be operated by the RAF, and were subsequently carried by the Vulcan, Buccaneer, Jaguar, Harrier and Tornado: the third variant was the RN depth charge version.

Vulcans, 'Micks' and 'Mickey Finns'

The Vulcan Operational Conversion Unit, No. 230 OCU, was formed at RAF Waddington in 1955, and received its first aircraft in July 1956.

The OCU took part in a series of record-breaking flights around the world that had the dual effects of waving of the Union Flag, as well as being a demonstration of Britain's nuclear capability. Flights from Waddington to Boston, USA, in 5 hours and 17 minutes, and to Cyprus in 3 hours and 41 minutes, showed the world that the RAF had a fast and effective means of delivering a retaliatory strike.

The OCU provided the aircraft for the first flight by an operational Vulcan squadron, No. 83, which took place in May 1957. By 1959, there were three Vulcan squadrons: apart from No. 83 at Waddington, No. 101 Squadron had formed at Finningley, and No. 617 Squadron had become the new residents at Scampton. Selection criteria

BELOW
Handley Page Victor B2 in anti-flash white colour scheme with its crew and Blue Steel stand-off bomb at RAF Wittering, Northants, 1964.

for the Vulcan aircrew was stringent: pilots were required to have at least 1,750 flying hours, and an 'above average' proficiency rating, while co-pilots needed to have each amassed at least 700 hours. Navigators and Air Electronics Officers (AEOs) were required to be 'experienced'.

Life on the V-bomber squadrons was punctuated by the frequent number of exercises that tested their readiness for action at short notice. In addition to 'scramble' alerts, there were often station alertness exercises that involved all personnel in a 'stand-to' at some deliberately chosen, anti-social time of day, usually in the early morning hours. Known as 'Mick', these exercises required the generation of the maximum number of serviceable aircraft, and arming them, within as

short a period as possible, culminating in a 'crew in' situation in which engines were sometimes started. This state fell short of the full-scale 'Mickey Finn' scenario, in which the aircraft were ordered to take off, and proceed to a nominated dispersed site, at any of the 36 airfields around the UK.

Living in temporary accommodation nearby their aircraft, the crew members awaited the 'scramble' call. When received, the Vulcan crews ran to their pre-checked aircraft, the AEO boarded first in order to start his equipment followed, in sequence, by the two pilots, then the two navigators. Engines were started while the crew strapped in, with the object of getting the aircraft onto the runway within two minutes. In most practice situations, the aircraft were not carrying a nuclear weapon.

The Versatile Victor

Deliveries of the Handley Page Victor B1 bomber began in November 1957, when No. 232 OCU became the first RAF unit to be equipped with this type. The following April, No. 10 Squadron became the first squadron to become operationally ready. The Victor's bomb bay was significantly larger than that of the other two V-bomber types, a feature demonstrated when it successfully carried, and later dropped, a total of thirty-five 1,000-pound bombs at one time. The Victor B1 and B1A versions continued in service, often being armed with the Yellow Sun nuclear weapon, until the mid-1960s when, by force of circumstance, its role was fundamentally changed. Some of the Victor B1 and B1A aircraft were converted, to perform tanker duties alongside the Vickers Valiant aircraft that were currently fulfilling that role.

As the Victor B2 version was entering service, there was a shift in policy from high-altitude bombing to the low-level, under-the-radar method of attack. The additional stresses imposed

at low-level had caused the onset of severe fatigue problems in the Valiant bombers that had also carried out the bulk of RAF air-to-air refuelling duties. The tanker availability situation became critically compromised when, in January 1965, it was discovered that the main spars in the Valiant airframes were seriously fatigued after performing low-level duties, for which they had not been designed, and all Valiants were immediately grounded.

Faced with a shortage of tanker capability, it was decided to hurriedly convert six of the Victor B1As to the 'two-point' tanker role. These were fitted with in-flight refuelling pods, one under each wing: later aircraft were fitted with an additional centreline pod, and became known as 'three-point' tankers. With the advent of the Victor B2 into operational bombing duties, the earlier versions that had been modified as tankers were re-designated K1 and K1A. Thus began a lengthy association with the airborne tanker role that was to last for almost thirty years, with the Victor K2s taking over from their earlier stable-mates. The Victor aircraft finally ended its service in 1993, with the disbandment of No. 55 Squadron at RAF Marham.

The Victor also proved to be a fine reconnaissance aircraft. Nine B2s were converted, during build, to become B(SR)2 aircraft. These

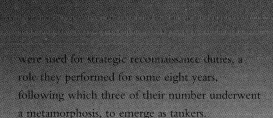

MAIN
The prototype TSR-2 that was a victim of cuts in defence spending in 1965.

were used for strategic reconnaissance duties, a role they performed for some eight years, following which three of their number underwent a metamorphosis, to emerge as tankers.

The TSR-2

Following the Labour government taking office in 1964, there was yet another review of Britain's defence expenditure. On Budget Day in 1965, Denis Healey, Secretary of State for Defence, announced that Britain would withdraw from its 'East of Suez' commitments. He also cancelled the BAC TSR-2 project, an expensive but 'cutting-edge of technology' Tactical/Strike/Reconnaissance (TSR) aircraft that was designed as a replacement for the Canberra bomber. The project was intended to provide an aircraft that could penetrate enemy airspace at low-level, and at very high speeds. It was to carry the most advanced avionics suite in the world, including Doppler radar, terrain-following radar

integrated with the flight control system, ground mapping radar, and a head-up flight-instrument display.

The TSR-2 was designed to be capable of delivering a large payload of conventional or nuclear weapons with greater accuracy, and with greater mission survivability, than any comparable aircraft envisaged at that time. The prototype had flown early in 1965, and the test flight program was progressing well. The second prototype was almost ready to join the test program when the project was cancelled, along with several other defence projects including new aircraft carriers for the Royal Navy.

Orders issued by the government, that required the destruction of jigs, drawings, and other items connected with TSR-2, gave the impression that there was a hidden political agenda behind the cancellation, other than that simply for reasons of finance. It was to be many years before the Royal Air Force would receive a single aircraft type that could perform all of the functions that the TSR-2 promised.

Chapter Eight

The 60s and 70s

Flash Points and Confrontation

Although the anti-terrorist campaign Operation Firedog came to its conclusion in July 1960 with the ending of the Malayan Emergency, the Royal Air Force was already involved in yet another flash point, this time in Africa. Transport Command's finest, in the guise of No. 216 Squadron with their deHavilland Comets, together with the Bristol Britannias of Nos. 99 and 511 Squadrons, were called upon to

don the 'metaphorical' blue berets of the United Nations. These squadrons provided transport for Ghanaian troops, leaving from Accra, for peacekeeping duties in the Congo. They were supported by Blackburn Beverleys of No. 30 Squadron, and subsequently, by the Handley Page Hastings of No. 114 Squadron, in the movement of troops and equipment within the Congo itself. Later, in September 1960, a detachment of Scottish Aviation Twin Pioneer aircraft and their crews from No. 230 Squadron were deployed elsewhere in Africa. On this occasion, the 'Twin Pins' lent their support to British Army

peacekeeping troops in the Cameroons, in the run-up to its constitutional reform.

Following Iraqi claims on its oil-rich neighbour Kuwait, the threat of invasion prompted the ruler of Kuwait to request British military support. Between July 1 and July 6 1961, the RAF flew 7,000 men, and 720 tons of supplies and equipment, into the Persian Gulf area from airfields in the United Kingdom, Cyprus, Aden and Kenya, in the reinforcement task called Operation Vantage. With two squadrons of ground-attack Hunter aircraft that were joined in the Persian Gulf area by Canberra bombers from Germany and with V-force aircraft at readiness in Malta, the deterrent force had the desired effect.

In 1962, as part of a South East Asia Treaty Organisation (SEATO) multinational task force, No. 20 Squadron fielded a detachment of its Hunter FGA9 aircraft to help to defend Thailand against a potential incursion by Pathet Lao, or North Vietnamese, troops. From their first location at Don Maung, near Bangkok, the RAF Tengah-based contingent subsequently transferred to Chiang Mai, in Northern Thailand, for a period of five months, during which time there were no incursions across the Thai border.

Triggered by events early in December 1962, there followed a period of instability in the Far East that was to last for almost four years. Sponsored by Indonesia, a revolt led by the North Kalimantan National Army (TNKU) attempted to depose the Sultan of Brunei. Britain responded by deploying Gurkha troops from RAF Seletar, Singapore to Brunei Town. Some of these troops were transported in three Blackburn Beverleys of No. 34 Squadron; a Britannia of No. 99 Squadron flew the remainder to Labuan. The RAF, using Hastings of No. 48 Squadron, Vickers Valettas of No. 52 Squadron, and Avro Shackletons of No. 205 Squadron, flew further troop reinforcements and equipment into the area. The Royal

Australian Air Force also assisted, using a Hercules of their No. 38 Squadron, as did the Royal New Zealand Air Force with a Bristol Freighter from their No. 41 Squadron.

RAF numbers increased with the arrival of detachments of Hunter FGA9s of No. 20 Squadron, and Canberra B15s of No. 45 Squadron, at Labuan, to provide close support. No. 209 Squadron's Twin Pioneer aircraft, supported by the Belvedere helicopters of No. 66 Squadron provided local air transport within Brunei. This prompt action by British and Commonwealth forces led to the collapse of the rebellion before Christmas, although there were ongoing, small-scale mopping-up operations for several months afterwards.

Following the creation of the Federation of Malaysia on September 16 1963, the Indonesian Confrontation began towards the latter part of 1963. Coupled with the desire of President Soekarno to expand Indonesia's territory into Malaysia and the Philippines, insurgents crossed the almost 1,000 mile border into Sarawak, Kalimantan, and Sabah. The Indonesian Air Force (AURI) also parachuted infiltrators into Singapore and mainland Malaysia.

The British response was to carry out intensive counter-insurgency operations in order to protect the new Federation. In support of the British Army, transport aircraft from the RAF moved men and equipment into the region. An Air Defence Identification Zone (ADIZ) was created over

MAIN
Vulcan B2 shortly
after takeoff.

Sarawak and Sabah, policed by Hawker Hunters from No. 20 Squadron, and Gloster Javelin fighters from Nos. 60 and 64 Squadron detachments, located at newly-created RAF Stations at Kuching and Labuan. As the political situation worsened, UK nationals were evacuated from Indonesia, around four hundred passengers being flown out to Singapore by No. 215 Squadron Argosy, and No. 48 Squadron Hastings, aircraft.

'Confrontation' lasted for almost four years, during which period many RAF personnel experienced the dubious pleasures of life as 'singlies' or 'lonely hearts' in the unpopular 'one year unaccompanied' tour of duty. Anybody who underwent the dubious pleasure of living in the Kuching Hilton (namely, a large tent!) soon became acquainted

with Borneo's wildlife, in particular its crawling and flying species, as well as the sauna-like humidity. Conditions improved dramatically with the move into a 'basha' hut billet, a design that was taken from the local Iban tribe's book on architecture.

In parallel with the conflict in the Far East, the RAF was also prominent in operations in the Middle East, as tensions heightened in the Aden Protectorate. In early January 1964, these tensions within Aden and the surrounding area reached a new high and, following a grenade attack on the British High Commissioner at Khormaksar, a state of emergency was declared. This resulted in Operation Nutcracker, in which the RAF and Fleet Air Arm gave air support to British Army units in the Radfan area. The conflict escalated to the extent that, in March 1964, armed helicopters from the Yemen, supported by MiG-17 fighters,

crossed the border and attacked the village of
Bulaq, and a frontier guard post. Royal Air Force
Hunters carried out a retaliatory raid, destroying a
Yemeni fort. In the following three months, the
Hunters flew 642 sorties in support of ground
forces, firing 2,508 rockets and 183,900 rounds of
ammunition in the process. Shackletons, carrying
out night bombing attacks, also flew support
missions while Beverley transport aircraft, together
with Belvedere and Whirlwind helicopters,
provided airlift and tactical transport for both
ground troops and their supplies.

The situation did not improve, even after the
British Government made the announcement that
it would grant independence to Aden, while
retaining a military base there. This news was
greeted by renewed fighting between the various
nationalist political factions, and attacks against the
security forces. In a change of mind by the British
Government in February 1966, it was decided that
Britain would not, after all, be retaining a military
base in Aden following its independence. This
precipitated a worsening in the security situation,
as those local factions that had previously been

MAIN
Wessex helicopter
supporting British
troops in Aden,
February 1966.

friendly towards the British administration gave vent to their dissatisfaction.

Terrorist attacks and public disorder continued until the commencement of the British withdrawal that began, in earnest, in November 1967. The withdrawal was to become the largest airlift operation carried out by the Royal Air Force since the Berlin Airlift of 1948-49. A total of 5,800 British Army personnel were flown out to RAF Muharraq, in the Persian Gulf, in a fleet of Hercules, Britannia, and Belfast aircraft of Transport Command. All locally based units were either relocated to bases within the Middle East, or disbanded; the withdrawal from Aden was completed by November 29 1967.

Meanwhile, RAF units were also occupied in Africa where, in January 1964, there had been a mutiny by five battalions of local troops within Tanganyika, Uganda and Kenya. Britain responded to requests for assistance, from the governments involved, by sending Belvedere helicopters from No. 26 Squadron that were used to transport No. 45 Commando, Royal Marines, from HMS Centaur to the barracks at Colito in Tanganyika, where they put down the rebellion. No. 30 Squadron sent Beverley transports to move 450 infantry troops from RAF Eastleigh, near Nairobi, in Kenya, to Entebbe in Uganda, to suppress the mutiny there.

Towards the end of 1964, No. 29 Squadron with its Javelin fighters was deployed from its base at RAF Akrotiri, to Ndola, to provide air defence cover for Zambia, where they remained until August 1966. This was in response to a Unilateral Declaration of Independence (UDI) by the Rhodesian government. Air defence radar systems and other equipment was flown into Zambia by Argosy transports of Nos. 114 and 267 Squadrons. Britain's attempt to blockade the illegal regime in Rhodesia also required it to provide support to Zambia's economy, namely, supplies of oil and petroleum products, by airlift, from Dar-Es-Salaam in Tanzania, Leopoldville in the Congo, and Nairobi in Kenya. This airlift was necessary because the usual rail link used for the transport of

such supplies from Mozambique passed through Rhodesian territory.

Assisted by Canadian forces, the airlift carried over 3.5 million gallons of oil products into Zambia. RAF Britannias of Nos. 99 and 511 Squadrons, and Hastings of Nos. 24 and 36 Squadrons participated in the airlift, which ended in October 1966. Shackletons of Nos. 37, 38, 42, 204, and 210 Squadrons, on rotation, and based temporarily at Majunga in Malagasy, assisted the Royal Navy in enforcing a blockade of the port of Beira, Mozambique, from March 1966 to February 1972. At home in Britain, an unusual operation involving Hunter aircraft from RAF Chivenor and West Raynham took place at the end of March 1967. Together with Buccaneers from the Fleet Air Arm, they took part in a series of rocket and bomb attacks on the tanker Torrey Canyon that had run aground on rocks of the Seven Stones Reef, near Land's End. The mission was to attempt to destroy the major part of the cargo of

BELOW
Extracts from booklet given to new arrivals at RAF Colerne, Wiltshire, circa 1964. It contained useful information on station regulations, sick parades and recreational facilities.

120,000 tons of crude oil that was causing severe pollution both in the sea, and on nearby beaches.

Northern Ireland was to become the focus of attention for Royal Air Force helicopter operations during the greater part of the next decade with the arrival in the province, in August 1970, of No. 72 Squadron with their Westland Wessex. Initially named Operation Marginal, this long-term deployment was renamed RAF Helicopter Detachment, Northern Ireland. The first RAF squadron to operate Puma helicopters, No. 33 Squadron, also served prominently in this theatre.

From May to November 1973, RAF aircraft undertook fishery surveillance flights over Icelandic waters in what became known as the 'Second Cod War'. Generally, Nimrod aircraft undertook these patrols but, unusually, to conserve airframe hours on the Nimrods, Britannia transport aircraft carried out some patrols. Another episode in the continuing 'Icelandic Cod Wars' saga in November 1975 again required the attentions of RAF Nimrod aircraft to help in the protection of British fishing vessels within the unilaterally-declared, 200-mile fishing prohibition zone around Iceland.

With the invasion of Northern Cyprus by Turkish troops in July 1974, British air defences in Cyprus were strengthened by the arrival of Phantom FGR2s of Nos. 6 and 41 Squadrons, and No. 228 OCU, some of the Phantoms remaining in Cyprus until September 1974. Defence of ground installations and RAF bases was bolstered by the arrival of RAF Regiment personnel from No. 15 and 26 Squadrons.

Following heightened tensions between Guatamala and Britain over the status of Belize, RAF Puma helicopters of No. 33 Squadron were flown to the colony in Belfast heavy-lift transport aircraft from No. 53 Squadron in October 1975. Further strengthening of defences, in order to deter any invasion by Guatamala, resulted in No. 1 Squadron Harriers also being detached to Belize

until the situation had normalised, when they returned to the UK in the following April. The year 1977 saw yet another deployment of No. 1 Squadron to the colony of Belize, following another breakdown in negotiations between Guatamala and Britain. On this occasion, the Harriers were flown to the colony with the assistance of Victor tankers. The Harrier detachment became a long-term commitment that resulted, in 1981, with it being designated No. 1417 Flight, and the Puma helicopter detachment becoming No. 1563 Flight.

Some Royal Air Force aircraft ended the 1970s as part of a cease-fire monitoring force in Rhodesia. Seven Hercules aircraft from No. 47 and 70 Squadrons, and six Puma helicopters from No. 33 Squadron, took part. Tragically, one of the Pumas, and its crew, were lost when it flew into overhead cables, only one day before the cease-fire came into effect.

Humanitarian and Relief Operations

During the period from 1961 to 1979, the RAF was often called upon to carry out a variety of relief operations caused by natural disasters such as floods, and in the aftermath of hurricanes and cyclones. In many locations around the world, from high in the Himalayas to the deserts of the Sahara, RAF aircraft and personnel have often been in the forefront of humanitarian efforts to ease the suffering of both the hungry, and the homeless.

October 1961 saw the combined efforts of RAF Transport Command and other Middle East-based units in Operation Tana. This involved the dropping of food supplies to communities that were isolated by floods, at first in Kenya, then later in Somalia. The following month, Operation Sky Help, called upon the RAF to, once again, spring into action after Hurricane Hattie had devastated large parts of British Honduras. Aircraft of both

Transport, and Coastal, Commands carried essential supplies between Kingston, Jamaica and Belize.

Elsewhere in the world, the RAF went about its usual business until November 1970, and again in June 1971, when relief efforts were put into operation to aid the population of East Pakistan, now known as Bangladesh. Following cyclones that resulted in heavy flooding along the coastal areas, the RAF mounted an emergency airlift of food and medical supplies into Chittagong. This operation involved the Hercules transport aircraft of No. 48 Squadron, from their base at RAF Changi, Singapore, and was the first time this aircraft type had been used for such a purpose while in RAF service. The ubiquitous Hercules, this time from RAF Lyneham, took to the mountains of Nepal during March 1973. Because of famine in West Nepal, and there being no suitable roads or airstrip, the dropping of emergency food supplies, by air, to the outlying villages was the only means of salvation for the population in this remote area.

In July 1974, following the invasion of Northern Cyprus by Turkish troops, RAF aircraft were used to evacuate British nationals to RAF Fairford and RAF Lyneham. The repatriation of service families followed in August, when a further evacuation of 9,989 dependants from RAF Akrotiri to the United Kingdom took place. This mammoth task was accomplished with the aid of volunteers, from all branches of the services, who assisted in the welfare of the unaccompanied families during their traumatic experience.

Long Distances, High Speeds, Short Times

The value of in-flight refuelling was demonstrated in several outstanding flights between the UK and its military bases in the Middle and Far East. As well as being important from the public relations aspect, it was also used as a more practical means of ensuring the rapid deployment of deterrent bomber forces over long distances. In May 1960, a Vickers Valiant of No. 214 Squadron made the first non-stop flight between the UK and Singapore. It covered the distance of 8,110 miles in 15 hours and 35 minutes, at an average speed of 623 miles per hour, and was twice refuelled in flight, first over Cyprus, and then near Karachi. Not to be outdone,

BELOW
Ground crew at work on a Lightning T5 of No. 56 Squadron at RAF Akrotiri, Cyprus. (© Crown Copyright)

an Avro Vulcan from No. 617 Squadron achieved the first non-stop flight between the United Kingdom and Australia on June 20-21 1961. Following three in-flight refuels, over Cyprus, Karachi and Singapore, respectively, it covered the distance of 11,500 miles in 20 hours and 3 minutes, at an average speed of 573 miles per hour.

The first round-the-world flight by the Vulcan took place in November 1962. One aircraft each from Nos. 27, 83, and 617 Squadrons made the circumnavigation in 50 hours flying time, with stopovers in Australia, New Zealand, and the USA.

New Aircraft and Equipment

Many new aircraft types or variants entered service with the RAF during the 1960s and 1970s. From the arrival of the Lightning F1 with No. 74 Squadron in 1960, there followed a succession of shiny debutantes onto the flight lines of stations throughout the UK and overseas. In 1961, two new types of helicopter, the Westland Whirlwind HAR10, and the twin-rotor Bristol Belvedere, entered service. The same year saw the arrival of the Hunter FR10, the Victor B2, and the Jet Provost T4. New types making their debut in 1962 were the deHavilland Comet C4 and Armstrong Whitworth Argosy transport aircraft, and the diminutive Folland Gnat trainer. A new variant of the Lightning, the F2, also entered service, with No. 19 Squadron. After a blank year, 1964 was notable for the entry into service of the Westland Wessex HC2 helicopter, the Hawker Siddeley Andover CC2 for The Queen's Flight, and the Lightning F3 for No. 74 Squadron.

Although not entering RAF operational squadron service the forerunner of the Harrier, the Hawker P1127 Kestrel, arrived at RAF West Raynham in 1964, where it joined a 'Tripartite Evaluation Squadron' to undergo trials by United Kingdom, German and United States forces.

The following year saw the Beagle Basset enter the hangar of the Northern Communications Squadron, the arrival of the Hawker Siddeley Dominie for No. 1 Air Navigation School, and the Lightning F6 for No. 5 Squadron. A year later, the latest incarnation of the Canberra, the T17 variant, was allocated to No. 39 Squadron. Transport Command was boosted by the arrival of the Andover C1, the Vickers VC10 C1, and the Short Belfast that incorporated the infamous 'bandstand' passenger seating arrangement located on a 'mezzanine' floor, from where the occupants were afforded a marvellous view of the cargo.

The service began to receive the Shorts Tigercat airfield defence surface-to-air missile system in 1966, to be operated by No. 48 Squadron, RAF Regiment. In the same year, following the cancellation of the TSR-2, the British Government ordered, as its replacement, a batch of 50 of the General Dynamics F111A variable geometry 'swing-wing' strike aircraft from the USA. This proved to be a 'false dawn' as this order was itself cancelled, less than two years later, before any of the type had entered service.

One aircraft design ordered from the USA that did enter service was the Lockheed C130K, known in the RAF as the Hercules C1. The first aircraft of a batch of 66 arrived at No. 242 OCU, RAF Thorney Island in 1967, and the type has continued to serve until well into the 21st century. Also acquired from the USA, but intended for a completely different purpose, the first of 118 McDonnell Douglas Phantom FGR2s went into RAF service in 1968 with No. 228 OCU, where crews were trained to fly this ground-attack and reconnaissance fighter.

The year 1969 saw aircraft types as varied as the Beagle Husky of No. 5 Air Experience Flight, the Harrier GR1 of No. 1 Squadron, the Jet Provost T5 of the Central Flying School, and the Phantom FG1 of No. 43 Squadron enter into service. They were joined in RAF service by the Hawker Siddeley Buccaneer for No. 12 Squadron, and the 'mighty hunter' Nimrod, from the same manufacturer, was taken on charge by No. 236 OCU. This spate of new machinery was followed by a lull, until 1971, when the Westland Puma arrived at No. 33 Squadron, and the BAe125 CC1 executive twin-jet set forth on the first of its VIP transport tasks with No. 32 Squadron.

Having had many of its alleged 'forty-thousand rivets flying in loose formation' tightened, and its airframe fitted with a prominent radar dome, the Avro Shackleton Airborne Early Warning (AEW) MR2 joined 'The Magic Roundabout' cast of characters at No. 8 Squadron in 1972. Each of the squadron's aircraft carried the name of a character from the popular children's television programme of the era, including the appropriately named 'Mr. Rusty'. This AEW version of the Shackleton was fitted with an APS 20 surveillance radar system that had originally been used in the Fleet Air Arm Gannet AEW3. The aircraft was intended as a 'stop-gap' measure following delays in the Nimrod AEW project that were to lead to its eventual cancellation. This supposedly short-term solution was to last for almost twenty years.

The Central Flying School received two new types in 1973, the Westland Gazelle helicopter and the Scottish Aviation Bulldog, while No. 5 Flying Training School acquired the Scottish Aviation Jetstream. Somewhat noisier, the Sepecat Jaguar also began to make itself seen, and heard, in the skies around its new home, the Jaguar OCU at RAF Coltishall, Norfolk, in 1974. In the same year, No. 51 Squadron received the first of its Nimrod R1 aircraft, at RAF Wyton, where it joined the squadron's specially modified Canberra aircraft on signals surveillance duties.

In 1975, the tanker force was strengthened by the arrival of the Victor K2 tanker for No. 55 Squadron at RAF Marham. A year later, the first

BAe Hawk T1 arrived at No. 4 FTS at RAF Valley, Anglesey. New metal, in the shape of the Andover E3 radar calibration aircraft that was to become a regular sight on the approach paths of RAF airfields for many years to come, joined No. 115 Squadron, at RAF Benson. During the latter years of the decade, deliveries of new aircraft types slowed to a trickle. When the Westland Sea King HAR3 joined No. 202 Squadron in 1978, all airmen whose favourite colour is yellow warmly welcomed it on arrival. This helicopter type has since taken part in many life-saving missions during a career that has stretched into the 21st century.

Notable events in 1977 included the participation of No. 208 Squadron's Buccaneers in the USAF exercise Red Flag at Nellis Air Force Base, Nevada. This was the first occasion that Royal Air Force aircraft and crews had been invited to take part in this event. Closer to home, a ceremonial flypast of Hercules aircraft took place at RAF Lyneham to celebrate the completion of 500,000 flying hours by 'Fat Albert' in RAF service.

Command and Organisation

The 1960s saw many changes in its operational and organisational arrangements. Britain's nuclear deterrent capability was frequently tested, usually on an annual basis, by 'Mickey Finn' dispersal exercises. A permanent V-bomber Quick Reaction Alert (QRA) capability was established in 1962; this required at least one aircraft from each operational squadron to be at 15 minutes readiness, at all times. The cancellation, by the Americans, of the ill-fated Skybolt project was seen by many as the beginning of the end for the air-launched ballistic nuclear weapon. Having selected a team of around 200 RAF personnel for Skybolt training at Eglin Air Force Base, Florida, in early 1962, the announcement by the United States of its intention to terminate the project, in December of that year, was greeted with disbelief in many circles.

Reorganisations and disbandments were rife during the 1960s and 1970s, both at home in the UK, and in several overseas RAF commands. In 1962, the first of the realignments and mergers that were to lead, eventually, to the formation of Strike Command in 1968, took place. This involved the transfer of two squadrons of Hunter fighter/ground-attack fighters, and some Canberra reconnaissance aircraft, to be placed under the control of No. 38 Group of Transport Command. Meanwhile, No. 2 Field Squadron, RAF Regiment, converted to the parachute role and the RAF College of Air Warfare arose, phoenix-like, from the ashes of the RAF Flying College. Overseas, the Headquarters, Near East Command was disbanded, permanently.

Elsewhere, Fighter Command's Nos. 11 and 12 Groups were disbanded, and replaced by three Sectors in early 1963. The Ballistic Missile Early Warning Station (BMEWS) was declared operational in September, and commenced operations in January 1964. During the summer of 1963, history was made when three Royal Standards were presented on one parade, to Nos.

203, 204, and 210 Squadrons, respectively, by Princess Margaret, at RAF Ballykelly, Northern Ireland.

On April 1 1964, a unified Ministry of Defence was created. New names were given to the existing components: the Air Ministry became the Air Force Department, the Air Council became the Air Force Board of the Defence Council, and the title of Secretary of State for Air changed to that of Minister of Defence for the Royal Air Force. The summer of that year was notable for the presentation of The Queen's

Colour for the Royal Air Force in the United Kingdom, by Her Majesty Queen Elizabeth II, at Buckingham Palace. Autumn time saw the ending of both the Aircraft Apprentice Scheme that was created in 1920, and the Boy Entrant Scheme that dated from 1934. These schemes were to be replaced by new Technician Apprentice, and Craft Apprentice Schemes, respectively.

The Defence White Paper of February 1964 gave three years notice of the merger of Flying Training and Technical Training Commands in 1968. The first Lightning squadron to be based

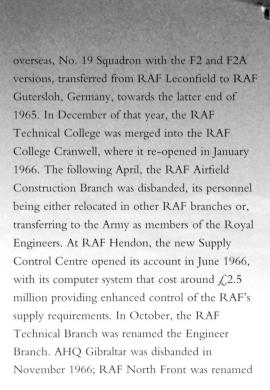

overseas, No. 19 Squadron with the F2 and F2A versions, transferred from RAF Leconfield to RAF Gutersloh, Germany, towards the latter end of 1965. In December of that year, the RAF Technical College was merged into the RAF College Cranwell, where it re-opened in January 1966. The following April, the RAF Airfield Construction Branch was disbanded, its personnel being either relocated in other RAF branches or, transferring to the Army as members of the Royal Engineers. At RAF Hendon, the new Supply Control Centre opened its account in June 1966, with its computer system that cost around £2.5 million providing enhanced control of the RAF's supply requirements. In October, the RAF Technical Branch was renamed the Engineer Branch. AHQ Gibraltar was disbanded in November 1966; RAF North Front was renamed

RAF Gibraltar, and was placed under the control of HQ 19 Group, Coastal Command.

Yet another Defence White Paper, issued in February 1967, foretold of the merger in April 1968 of Bomber and Fighter Commands, with No. 1 (Bomber) Group HQ at RAF Bawtry, and No. 11 (Fighter) Group HQ at RAF Bentley Priory, replacing the two former commands within the new Strike Command. Later in the same year, RAF Transport Command was renamed RAF Air Support Command and given a wider responsibility in the tactical support/assault roles, in addition to its long-range strategic transport function. HQ RAF Persian Gulf was renamed Headquarters, Air Forces Gulf which, in turn, was to become the air component of the

MAIN
Lightning F6 fitted with over-wing long-range fuel tanks.

new HQ, British Forces Gulf, based in Bahrein, just two months later in November 1967.

January 1968 began with sweeping cuts in Britain's defences. These included the cancellation of the contract for 50 General Dynamics F111 aircraft, and the withdrawal of British forces from the Persian Gulf and the Far East by December 1971, as well as increasing the rate of the reduction in numbers of RAF personnel. The RAF would inherit most of the fixed-wing aircraft from the Fleet Air Arm, as the RN carrier fleet

was to be phased out. Meanwhile, RAF Training Command was resurrected as a result of the merger of Flying Training, and Technical Training, Commands. The year also saw the disappearance of the title of RAF Coastal Command, as it was absorbed into RAF Strike Command with the designation No. 18 (Maritime) Group.

In June 1968, RAF Abingdon was the setting for a Royal Review of the Royal Air Force by Queen Elizabeth II to mark the 50th anniversary of the formation of the service. The year of 1969 was ushered in with RAF Signals Command being disbanded, and re-branded as No. 90 (Signals) Group, Strike Command. Also in January, a formal disbandment parade was held prior to the imminent demise of Nos. 6, 32, 73, and 249 Squadrons of the Near East Air Force Strike Wing, that would follow within the first two months of that year. They were to be replaced by a new Strike Wing, at RAF Akrotiri, comprising Nos. 9 and 35 Squadrons, each with eight Vulcan B2 bombers.

As tensioned heightened in the province, RAF helicopters were detached to Northern Ireland in July 1969. The detachment was formed firstly by Wessex helicopters from No. 72 Squadron, and later, from No. 18 Squadron when they arrived in March 1970. A much-anticipated journey to sunnier climes was in store for some of its fighter squadrons as the RAF began to use the new Air Weapons Training Installation at Decimomannu in Sicily, in January 1970. This was a state-of-the-art, fully instrumented, air combat training facility that enabled real-time, as well as post-flight, analysis of fighter combat techniques.

A sad loss occurred on February 15, when the death was announced of Air Chief Marshal Sir Hugh Dowding, aged 87, who had commanded Fighter Command during the Battle of Britain. In March, in response to a request by the new government of Libya, that had taken power in a coup in the previous September, the RAF withdrew from its base at El Adem. Between April and June, the RAF featured prominently in the first major, multilateral military exercise in the Far East. Known as Bersatu Padu, loosely translated as 'Staying together, moving ahead', this exercise involved personnel and equipment from the UK, Australia, New Zealand, Malaysia, and Singapore, in which a total of over 200 aircraft, 50 ships and 20,000 men took part.

The final withdrawal from RAF bases in the Far East led to the disbanding of the Far East Air Force in October 1971, while a similar fate awaited Air Forces Gulf in the December of that year. Yet another round of mergers and transfers took place in 1972: No. 90 (Signals) Group was transferred from Strike Command to Maintenance Command, and No. 38 Group, Air Support Command came under the control of Strike Command, and was designated No. 46 Group. On November 15 1972, Queen Elizabeth II opened the RAF Museum at Hendon, the site being chosen for both its historical heritage, and its location.

RAF Maintenance Command disbanded on August 31 1973, its functions being absorbed into the new RAF Support Command which formed the next day. Following the Turkish invasion of Cyprus in the previous year, January 1975 saw major changes in Cyprus. All RAF fixed-wing assets were withdrawn to the UK and re-deployed within Strike Command, leaving RAF Akrotiri almost bereft of aircraft, except for the helicopters of No. 84 Squadron, and UK-based transport aircraft staging through en-route. The Near East Air Force disbanded on March 31 1976 prior to the formation of AHQ Cyprus, under the control of Strike Command, a day later. At home, the strategic transport assets of No. 46 Group were combined under the nameplate of No. 38 Group, Strike Command.

The staging post at RAF Gan, in the Maldive Islands, finally closed in 1976 after almost twenty years establishment as a vital part of the service's transport network. In the following year, a Silver Jubilee Review of the Royal Air Force was carried out by Queen Elizabeth II, at RAF Finningley, Yorkshire. As the decade neared its close, so did the RAF presence on the island of Malta: on March 31 1979, it withdrew, ending an association that had lasted for 60 years.

RIGHT
An aircraft being refuelled at RAF Gan, in the Maldives, 1962. Later to become a tourist resort, Gan was described as 'the RAF's own island in the sun' in some contemporary recruiting advertisements!

Chapter Nine

War and the Peace Dividend

At the start of the 1980s, the Royal Air Force participated in the United Nations Cease-fire Monitoring Force in Rhodesia that continued until April 1980, when the force was disbanded. That year was also the 40th anniversary of the Battle of Britain and was celebrated with a public air show at RAF Coltishall, Norfolk, the last remaining operational station of the battle.

At the beginning of 1981, the first course at the new Tri-national Tornado Training

Establishment commenced training at RAF Cottesmore, with the station hosting trainee Tornado crews from Germany and Italy, in addition to those from the RAF.

In June 1980, the government announced the intention to purchase 60 McDonnell Douglas AV8B aircraft for the RAF. This procurement was effectively 'taking coals to Newcastle' in the sense that Britain was purchasing an American development of the erstwhile British Harrier that was to be designated Harrier GR5. The following November saw the return to Northern Ireland of No. 72 Squadron with their Westland Wessex helicopters, a reprise of their detachment in the province that had lasted for much of the previous decade. Other Wessex aircraft, this time in the yellow of the SAR version, fulfilled that role with Nos. 22 and 202 Squadrons as their smaller, shorter-range Westland Whirlwind helicopters were retired from service.

The Falklands War 1982

The invasion of the Falkland Islands by the forces of Argentina in Operation Rosario, on April 2 1982, triggered the expected military response by Britain that was named Operation Corporate. The Royal Air Force was immediately called upon, and sent four Hercules transport aircraft to RAF Gibraltar. These aircraft were to form part of a supply chain, for personnel and equipment, between Britain and the forward operating base at Wideawake Air base on Ascension Island, in the South Atlantic. A day later, a VC10 of No. 10 Squadron from RAF Brize Norton was despatched to Montevideo, in Uruguay, to collect the British Governor of the Falkland Islands, and a party of Royal Marines, captured by Argentine forces during the invasion of the islands they referred to as 'Las Malvinas.' The VC10s continued to operate between Montevideo and the UK, and flew many casualties from the conflict back to Britain.

Chapter Nine

Two Nimrod MR1 aircraft from No. 42 Squadron left RAF St. Mawgan for Ascension Island where they were engaged in long-range patrols in support of the British Task Force, supplemented by Nimrod MR2s from Nos. 120, 201 and 206 Squadrons. Later, on April 18, five

Wessex helicopters in bad weather while attempting to evacuate Special Air Service troops from South Georgia.

Following the imposition by Britain of a 200-mile radius 'no-fly' zone around the Falklands, it became apparent that the Task Force was about to take the first punitive action against the occupying

Victor K2 tankers from No. 55 and 57 Squadrons arrived at Wideawake, from where they were initially engaged in maritime radar reconnaissance flights over the South Atlantic, around the islands of South Georgia and the Falklands. On one such mission, a radar patrol by a Victor covered some 150,000 square miles of ocean in 14 hours and 45 minutes. Just three days later, the RAF lost two

forces. In preparation, the first Vulcan B2 bombers from the Waddington Wing, comprising Nos. 44, 50 and 101 Squadrons, arrived at Ascension Island on April 29. The first offensive sortie of the campaign took place over the two days of April 30 and May 1. In the longest-range bombing sortie up to that period, the mission Black Buck 1, flown

MAIN
A Rapier low level air defence (LLAD) missile leaving its launcher. The system was credited with 14 kills and six probables, from a total of 24 missiles fired, during the Falklands Campaign.

by Vulcan B2 XM 607, and supported by eighteen Victor K2 tanker sorties, dropped twenty-one 1,000-pound bombs across the runway at Port Stanley. The Vulcan returned safely to the Ascension Island base after a flight time of 15 hours and 45 minutes. This attack on Port Stanley airfield was followed-up by Fleet Air Arm Sea Harriers, with a further attack on the airstrip at Goose Green.

Two days later on May 3 and 4, the second Vulcan attack, Black Buck 2, dropped a further twenty-one 1,000-pound bombs on the airfield at Port Stanley. Although later reconnaissance showed that these had landed close to the runway, the damage caused by the previous attack was still un-repaired. Black Buck 3 and 4 missions were flown on May 31 and June 4, in which Shrike anti-radar missiles were launched against Argentine Skyguard installations on the Falklands. During Black Buck 4, the Vulcan sustained damage to its refuelling probe and diverted to Rio de Janeiro, Brasil, where it was impounded until June 10. The final mission, Black Buck 5 on June 12, was made using 1,000-pound bombs directed against concentrations of Argentine troops near Port Stanley. Although it was subsequently shown that the Black Buck operations had little direct military effect on the outcome of the Falklands War, there were several indirect benefits. As well as providing a 'morale boosting' effect on the British population of the Falklands, there was an opposite effect on the morale of the Argentine military forces of occupation. The theatre of operations also highlighted the need for the provision of an in-flight refuelling capability in those Royal Air Force combat and transport aircraft that were, as yet, not fitted with the necessary systems. The provision and installation of such equipment, at very short notice, tested the ingenuity of both the British aircraft industry and the engineering staff of the RAF.

On May 7, the first Nimrod to be fitted with an in-flight refuelling probe was deployed to Wideawake Air Base. Subsequently, this MR2P variant, XV227, of No. 206 Squadron became the first Nimrod to carry out an extended anti-submarine patrol with in-flight refuelling. The next day, a Westland Sea King HAR3 of No. 202 Squadron was flown to Ascension in an ex-RAF Belfast transport aircraft operated by the civil company Heavylift, to provide both Search And Rescue (SAR) cover, and also local transportation, around the island. This coincided with the arrival, on the same day, of a combined force of twenty Harriers and Sea Harriers at Ascension, after a non-stop flight of around nine hours, that included several in-flight refuels, from RNAS Yeovilton, Somerset. A further six RAF Harrier GR3s from No. 1 Squadron arrived in the South Atlantic by sea, aboard the container ship Atlantic Conveyor, from

where they flew to join their naval cousins, the Sea Harriers of No. 809 Squadron, RNAS, aboard the aircraft carrier HMS Hermes.

On May 19, the only fatality suffered by the Royal Air Force during the campaign occurred in a flying accident not resulting from enemy action. Flight Lieutenant G.W. Hawkins, a Forward Air Controller, lost his life when the Sea King helicopter, in which he was a passenger, crashed into the sea after a suspected bird strike. Twenty of the total of twenty-nine personnel on board lost their lives.

The first attack of the campaign by the Harrier GR3 was a successful cluster bomb raid against a

fuel dump at Fox Bay in West Falkland, on May 20, in which three of the No. 1 Squadron aircraft took part, with no RAF casualties. To protect the Wideawake base against attack by the Argentine Air Force, three McDonnell Douglas Phantom FGR2 aircraft of No. 29 Squadron were deployed to Ascension by May 26, for QRA defence duties, where they remained until late in July.

On May 21, following SAS intelligence reports that Argentine helicopters had been hidden in a hollow between Mount Kent and Mount Estancia, two Harrier GR3s of No. 1 Squadron from HMS Hermes set off at first light. One of the helicopters, a Bell UH-1D Huey, was already airborne at the time of the attack, and made good its escape. The remaining two Pumas and a Chinook were hit by 30mm cannon rounds from the Harriers, and caught fire. One of the Harriers

BELOW
Nimrod receiving fuel from a Victor tanker.

NEXT PAGE
Phantom refuelling from a Hercules tanker.

was hit by three bullets from ground fire but returned safely to HMS Hermes. On the same day, the RAF lost its first Harrier when a GR3 of No. 1 Squadron was shot down, probably by a surface-to-air missile. Its pilot, Flight Lieutenant Glover, ejected successfully but was injured and subsequently taken prisoner. After treatment at Comodoro Rivadavia on the Argentine mainland, he was eventually repatriated on July 8, after all hostilities had ceased.

One of the blackest days of the operation for British forces was May 25 1982. The events of this day led to the loss of two vessels from its Task Force. The first of these losses was that of the Royal Navy's Type 42-destroyer HMS Coventry when she was sunk following a bombing attack by Argentine Air Force Skyhawk aircraft. The second Task Force loss occurred when the Atlantic Conveyor went to the bottom of the Atlantic Ocean, after being hit by an Exocet missile fired from an Argentine Navy Dassault Super Etandard aircraft. Her cargo, including three RAF Chinook helicopters and a further six RN helicopters, went down with her.

The second Harrier GR3 to be lost in the conflict was shot down by radar-controlled anti-

damage caused a fuel shortage that prevented the aircraft from returning to HMS Hermes; the pilot, Squadron Leader Pook, ejected safely into the sea and was rescued. RAF pilots were also active in the Sea Harrier force. One of these, Flight Lieutenant D. Morgan, became the top scoring British pilot of the campaign, shooting down four Argentinean aircraft, an achievement for which he was awarded the Distinguished Service Cross.

During the Falklands War, RAF transport aircraft played a significant role in the supply chain to both Ascension Island, and onward to the occupied territory. Within the Falklands, one of the most important contributions to the British effort was afforded by the lone surviving Chinook helicopter of No. 18 Squadron that had operated, initially, without spares or tools that had been sunk with the Atlantic Conveyor.

Major contributions were made by the VC10s and Hercules aircraft that ferried men and equipment between the UK, Ascension Island and the Falklands, known in RAF circles as 'down South'. Some of the Hercules had been hurriedly modified with internal long-range fuel tanks, and also fitted with in-flight refuelling probes, in order

aircraft gunfire on May 27, near Goose Green. Its pilot, Squadron Leader Bob Iveson, ejected safely, hid away, and was later rescued by helicopter. Three days later, another Harrier GR3 was hit by ground fire near Port Stanley. The resulting

to extend their range. Others were also converted to provide tanker facilities via a refuelling hose and drogue system fitted through the modified cargo bay door.

Although too late for use in the conflict, these tankers provided valuable facilities for

garrison defence fighters in the post-war period following the surrender of Argentine troops on June 14 1982.

Lull before the Storm

Following the conflict in the South Atlantic, the RAF helicopter inventory was augmented by the formation of a second Chinook squadron, No. 7 Squadron, at RAF Odiham, in September 1982. Air defence duties in the Falklands were taken over by the Phantom FGR2s of No. 29 Squadron, until October of the following year when No. 23 Squadron took over the responsibility. At home, July 1983 saw the first Lockheed Tristar tanker/transport aircraft enter service with No. 216 squadron at RAF Brize Norton, this station also receiving the first Vickers VC10 K2 tankers for No. 101 Squadron during the same month. Toward the end of 1983, a detachment of Chinook helicopters from No. 7 and 18 Squadrons supported a British Army peacekeeping force in Lebanon, while Buccaneers from Nos. 12 and 208 Squadrons provided offensive backup from RAF Akrotiri in Cyprus.

RAF Hercules made humanitarian relief flights in Ethiopia, as part of Operation Bushel, at the end of 1985. These provided an emergency airlift of food and other essential supplies following both famine and the further indignity to the population caused by civil war. More than 2,000 sorties were flown to either air drop or air-land more than 32,000 tonnes of aid to the stricken area.

Desert Shield and Desert Storm

Iraqi forces invaded and occupied Kuwait on August 2 1990. Four days later, King Fahd of Saudi Arabia requested military support from governments that were friendly towards his country. The United States and United Kingdom governments responded, and the RAF involvement in Operation Granby, as it was designated by Britain, commenced almost immediately. By August 11, British combat aircraft were arriving in the Gulf area in the form of twelve Tornado F3 air defence fighters that had, fortuitously, been attending an Armament Practice Camp at RAF Akrotiri. Two days later, twelve Jaguar GR1A ground attack aircraft from RAF Coltishall arrived in Thumrait, Oman, prior to being re-deployed one month later, to Muharraq, in Bahrain.

The Saudi Arabian airfield at Dhahran soon began to fill with RAF personnel and equipment, brought by RAF Hercules and Tristar transports. The air base at Seeb, in Oman, saw the arrival of two VC10 tankers from No. 101 Squadron, and three Nimrod MR2 aircraft. The build-up continued with the arrival, at Muharraq, of a Tornado GR1 detachment from Germany, at the end of August, with further deployments of Tornado GR1s at Tabuk and Dhahran by the first week in January 1991. Meanwhile, at the beginning of November, a detachment of Hercules from Lyneham was established at King Khalid International Airport, Riyadh. Shortly before Christmas 1990, the first four aircraft, of a total of eight Victor tankers, arrived in Muharraq, the remainder arriving early in January. RAF assets in the area were further boosted by the arrival of a reconnaissance detachment of six Tornado GR1As at Dhahran on January 14 1991.

Operation Desert Storm began on January 16-17 1991 with an air assault on Iraqi airfields and key military installations. The first RAF attacks on Iraqi airfields were carried out using a variety of ordnance, including 1,000-pound bombs and Hunting JP233 airfield denial munitions. The first RAF loss due to enemy action occurred when a Tornado was shot down by a surface-to-air missile after a low-altitude bombing attack on Ar Rumaylah air base in Southern Iraq; its crew ejected, and both taken prisoner. They were

beaten, tortured, and later paraded on television by their captors, who showed no respect for the Geneva Convention regarding the treatment of prisoners of war. Another Tornado was shot down on January 18 with the fatal loss of both of its crew. In total, six Tornado GR1s were lost in the campaign; of the total of twelve aircrew members, five men made the ultimate sacrifice, giving their lives to the cause.

With continuing attacks on Iraqi Scud missile sites and other critical targets, the RAF Tornadoes, Jaguars and Buccaneers made valuable contributions to the war effort, with support from other RAF resources including the medical, logistics, airfield defence, and communications specialisations. Aerial offensive sorties continued as preparations for the ground offensive were under way. The Allies successfully cut all the main supply routes to the beleaguered Iraqi ground troops, including bridges, rail-links and highways. The war to regain Kuwait was effectively won after a four-day ground assault, when hostilities officially ceased on February 29 1991.

The Balkans

On March 31 1993, RAF assets were deployed as part of a NATO force in Operation Deny Flight that was set up to police a 'no-fly' zone over Bosnia. This involved RAF Tornado F3s, Boeing Sentry AEW1s and Jaguars, supported by VC10 tankers. RAF Hercules provided an airlift of humanitarian aid and supplies into the area, and also took part in the evacuation of casualties from Sarajevo to Britain, for specialised medical treatment. Due to the ongoing and escalating problems in the area, the NATO forces commenced Operation Deliberate Force on August 30 1995, in an effort to protect the population of the Sarajevo area. In the following two weeks, Royal Air Force aircraft flew 268 sorties in which they dropped thirty-two 1,000-

pound bombs, and forty-eight laser-guided bombs, against twenty-two targets. Subsequently, in December 1995, three RAF Chinook helicopters formed part of the Support Helicopter Force, based at Split, in Croatia, from where they assisted a multi-national force to implement the Dayton Peace Accord.

For the next three years there was continued involvement by the Royal Air Force in the former Yugoslavia. In March 1999, following the breakdown in diplomatic efforts to impose a settlement over the status of the province of

Kosovo, NATO forces took part in Operation Allied Force that was intended to force the withdrawal of Serbian troops from the province. The NATO strategy was to carry out an intensive, and systematic, bombing campaign against Serbian forces in Kosovo, and also against key targets within Serbia itself. The RAF was involved in Operation Allied Force from the outset. On the first night of the operation, March 24 1999, six BAe Harrier GR7 aircraft, supported by Lockheed Tristar tankers and Boeing Sentry Airborne Early Warning aircraft, participated in an attack on an

MAIN
Lockheed Tristar delivers fuel to a Vickers VC10. The receiving aircraft is in one of several different colour schemes used on the VC10 in RAF service.
(© Crown Copyright)

ammunition store in Serbia. The attack was aborted due to smoke over the objective that had prevented the laser-guided bombs from locking onto their designated targets.

On April 4 and 5 1999, six Tornado GR1s from RAF Bruggen in Germany, supported by VC10 tankers also operating from Bruggen, attacked bridges and tunnels on the Serbian supply routes into Kosovo. One month later, twelve Tornado GR1s were deployed to the French Air force base at Solenzara, in Corsica, from where they were to participate in Allied Force. Shortly

after carrying out their first offensive operation, NATO suspended air operations against Serbian forces, both within Kosovo and against Serbia itself, on June 10. Following the suspension of air attacks by NATO forces, and rigorous diplomatic activity, Serbian forces began to withdraw from Kosovo on June 12. RAF helicopters, including six Pumas and eight Chinooks, took part in Operation Agricola wherein British troops were deployed into Kosovo in the largest support helicopter deployment since Operation Granby in the 1990 Gulf War. By the third week in June

1999, Serbian troops had completed their withdrawal, and a NATO peacekeeping force was in place in Kosovo to both maintain order and create a stable and secure background for regeneration of the province.

Iraq Revisited – Desert Fox and the No-Fly Zones

Operation Desert Fox was intended to both degrade the infrastructure associated with Iraq's ability to manufacture and deploy weapons of 'mass destruction', and reduce the Iraqi military capability for aggression against its neighbouring states, including Israel. Following air-strikes and cruise missile attacks by United States forces against targets in Iraq on December 16 and 17 1998, Royal Air Force Tornado GR1s left their base in Kuwait to attack military targets near Basra.

During the first two months of 1999, RAF Tornadoes from Nos. 2 and 12 Squadrons flew many sorties against military installations, including Iraqi ground-radar sites that were known to be tracking British and American aircraft policing the 'No-Fly' zone in southern Iraq. In many cases, the Paveway laser-guided bomb was used against these targets, more than 60 being dropped by No. 12 Squadron in the month of January.

Landmarks and Milestones in the 1980s and 1990s

Organisational changes continued with the amalgamation, in November 1983, of Strike Command's Nos. 1 and 38 Groups into No. 1 Group. However, this was a far from permanent merger as No. 38 Group was reformed in November 1992.

A significant event in the procurement process for a new combat aircraft took place on December 16 1983, when a preliminary agreement for the development of a Future European Fighter Aircraft was signed by the Chiefs of Staff of air forces from Britain, France, Germany, Italy and Spain. The following year, on March 31 1984, the Royal Air Force bade farewell to its last serving Avro Vulcan

when No. 50 Squadron disbanded at RAF Waddington, Lincolnshire. Later that year, the first two Tornado F2s arrived at No. 229 Operational Conversion Unit at RAF Coningsby.

Notable among the new aircraft entering RAF service during the 1980s and 1990s were the following types:

- Lockheed Hercules C3 and Panavia Tornado GR1 (1980).
- Boeing Chinook (1981).
- Lockheed Tristar (1983).
- McDonnell Douglas Phantom F3 and British Aircraft Corporation VC10 K2 (1984).
- British Aerospace 146 (1986).
- BAe Harrier GR5 and Panavia Tornado F3 (1987).
- Short Tucano (1989).
- British Aerospace Harrier GR7 (1990).
- Boeing Sentry AEW1 (1991).
- Slingsby Firefly (1993).
- Bell Griffin HT1 (1997).
- Lockheed Hercules C4 (1999).

The Royal Air Force finally severed its connection with the sea when the Marine Branch was disbanded on 1 April 1986. This Branch had served for many years as part of the Search and Rescue (SAR) service, both in peacetime and in war, saving the lives of many pilots that had ditched or parachuted into the sea. Its vessels also provided safety patrols around coastal weapons ranges, and target towing facilities.

A New Peace in Europe

On April 1 1993, Queen Elizabeth II carried out a Royal Review of the Royal Air Force on the 75th anniversary of its foundation, at RAF Marham. This anniversary also marked the official disbandment of RAF Germany and the formation of No. 2 Group, Strike Command, at RAF Rheindahlen. The new Group was established to oversee the remainder of the RAF assets in Germany until 1996, when this, the last headquarters unit of the RAF on mainland Europe, finally closed. The military rundown, and subsequent withdrawal of the Royal Air Force from mainland Europe, heralded a new peace throughout the continent that was now free from the implicit threat previously imposed by the armed forces of the Soviets and their Eastern-bloc allies.

Later in 1996, the RAF retired both the Buccaneer strike aircraft and the last of the Victors that had served first as a bomber, and later a tanker, for 36 years. The sole surviving 'women only' service organisation, The Women's Royal Air Force (WRAF), disbanded on April 1 1994. Amalgamation and inter-service co-operation went hand-in-hand as the RAF Staff College at Bracknell closed on December 31 1996, to be replaced on the same site by the new Joint Services Command and Staff College.

The last remaining Royal Air Force station in Asia, RAF Sek Kong in the New Territories, Hong Kong, finally closed in January 1997, in preparation for the hand over of Hong Kong to China. The last flying RAF squadron in the Far East, No. 28 Squadron, temporarily transferred to the Hong Kong civil airport until withdrawing from the area in June 1997.

Further organisational changes took place in April 1997 with the implementation of the Reserve Forces Act; this called for a single RAF reserve force. The Royal Auxiliary Air Force (RAuxAF) was to fill this requirement, with the members of the

BELOW
Harrier GR7.

Royal Air Force Volunteer Reserve (RAFVR) being integrated into it on the disbandment of their organisation, after 60 years of existence. At the same time, the Operations Support Branch was created to combine the existing specialist elements of air traffic control, fighter control, intelligence, and RAF Regiment, together with the newly created 'flight operations' specialisation. Also in April, the Defence Helicopter Flying School (DHFS) opened at RAF Shawbury where, apart from absorbing the flying training element of No. 2 Flying Training School, it also took over the Search and Rescue Training School.

The Female Achievers

In 1987, at RAF College Cranwell, the first award of the Queen's Medal to a female officer, for the most outstanding officer cadet of the year, was made to Flight Officer Susan Forbes of the Engineering Branch.

Although women in the RAF had previously served in its aircraft as cabin crew, a new policy statement made in Parliament on July 20 1989 announced that females should be allowed to fly as aircrew, in all categories including that of pilot, in non-combat roles. They were not, at this stage, to be accepted for flying duties in the fast-jet, support helicopter, or maritime reconnaissance roles. Subsequently, on May 10 1990, Flight Lieutenants Julie Ann Gibson and Sally Cox become the first female pilots to fly solo in a Royal Air Force jet aircraft, when they each flew alone in a Jet Provost training aircraft at No. 1 Flying Training School, RAF Linton-on-Ouse. Flight Lieutenant Gibson later became the first female regular officer to graduate as a pilot, when she was awarded her wings on June 14 1991. The Royal Air Force's first female navigator, Flying Officer Anne-Marie Dawe, graduated from No. 6 Flying Training School, RAF Finningley, on March 1 1991, and was subsequently posted

to No. 242 Operational Conversion Unit, RAF Lyneham.

The restriction that precluded female aircrew from flying support helicopters and maritime reconnaissance aircraft was lifted during 1991 followed, in December 1991, with the announcement that fast-jet seats would now be available to female pilots and navigators. Resulting from this, Flight Lieutenant Sally Cox joined the fast-jet students, the first female to do so, on No. 128 Course at No. 2 Tactical Weapons Unit, RAF Chivenor on January 14 1992. The first female Royal Air Force helicopter pilot, Flight Lieutenant Nicky Smith, graduated from No. 89 Course at No. 2 Flying Training School, RAF Shawbury, on October 16 1992. The Royal Air Force's first female, combat-ready, fast-jet pilot, Flight Lieutenant Jo Salter (later Ashfield, on marriage),

joined No. 617 Squadron to fly the Tornado GR1B at RAF Lossiemouth in August 1994.

The Strategic Defence Review 1997

Once again the RAF, together with the Army and Royal Navy, faced the imposed task of re-organisation, in response to policy changes, that were included in the 1997 Strategic Defence Review (SDR) by the newly elected Labour Government. Among the changes in front-line operations was the announcement that Royal Navy Sea Harrier units, together with those operating the RAF Harrier GR7s, would be merged to form Joint Force Harrier. This force was to operate from either RN Invincible Class carriers, or from shore bases, as necessary. On the final retirement of the Sea Harrier in 2006, Joint Force Harrier would operate the GR7 and upgraded GR9 versions of the Harrier until the new American F-35 Joint Strike Fighter enters service. All helicopters used in battlefield support operations, some four hundred in number, were also to be combined to form a new Joint Helicopter Command.

One of the keywords of the SDR was 'mobility'. This led to the formation of a Joint Rapid Reaction Force that could be deployed at short notice. The SDR recognised the requirement for a strategic transport force, the Royal Air Force requirement being filled, in the short term, by the lease of four Boeing C-17 Globemaster aircraft, that were later to be purchased outright. Future transport needs were to be met with the purchase 'off the drawing board' (or, more correctly, off the computer screen) of the Airbus A400M. However, this aircraft would not enter RAF service until late in the first decade of the new Millennium, at the earliest.

The RAF was, once again, required to undergo a further 'shrinkage' or 'downsizing' that was part and parcel of the many previous defence 'reviews' it had undergone over the years. Its 'fast jet' force was to be reduced by two squadrons, around 36 aircraft, although the Eurofighter project was to continue. There was also an acknowledged requirement for a Tornado GR4 replacement. The procurement of armaments such as the Storm Shadow stand-off attack missile, that entered service in 2002, and the Brimstone anti-armour missile, in service in 2004, improved the RAF's strike capability. The Meteor 'Beyond-Visual Range Air-to-Air Missile' (BVRAAM), that is a collaboration with several European countries, is not expected to be available for use by the RAF's Eurofighter Typhoons until at least 2012. Until such time as Meteor enters service, the Typhoon will be armed with the Advanced Medium Range Air-to-Air Missile (AMRAAM).

The SDR recommended that the retirement of the WE.177 tactical nuclear weapon should be accelerated. This event occurred on March 31 1998, when the last 'bucket of instant sunshine' was withdrawn from RAF service. Looking toward the possibility of being on the receiving end of the nuclear threat, the review called for the creation of an integrated Nuclear Biological Chemical (NBC) force, comprising both regular and reserve forces from the Army and the RAF, that would specialise in NBC defensive capabilities. This force came into being in 1999 with the formation of the Joint NBC Regiment.

In the aftermath of the September 11th 2001 terrorist attacks on New York and Washington, Geoff Hoon, the Secretary of State for Defence, announced a further Chapter of the Strategic Defence Review (SDR). This would entail a review of the UK's defence plans following the 9/11 attacks, as they became known. These plans included, amongst others, the placing of RAF air defence assets on QRA standby, in order to counter any potential terrorist aerial attack on the UK, including the use of hijacked civilian aircraft.

RIGHT
No. 13 Squadron Tornado GR4A is capable of carrying Storm Shadow, shown here, and Brimstone weapons. (© Crown Copyright)

Chapter Ten

Chapter Ten

Into the Future

The Royal Air Force in the 21st Century

The new millennium saw the delivery, in February 2000, of the first Panavia Tornado GR4 to No. 617 Squadron. This version of the Tornado, with its updated and advanced avionics and weapon systems is expected to remain in service with the RAF for a further twenty years. The new Joint Forces Air Command Headquarters began limited operations at RAF High Wycombe at the beginning of March, to be followed a month later by the new Joint Force Harrier which commenced operations with its headquarters at RAF Wittering, and its aircraft based at RAF Cottesmore.

On May 16 2000 came the formal announcement of the leasing of four Boeing C-17 Globemaster III transports, and the intention to purchase twenty-five Airbus A400M aircraft, to replace the ageing Hercules C130K variant, for entry into RAF service in 2009. It was also announced that the Eurofighter Typhoon would not be armed with cannon, although the first batch of forty would be fitted with cannon but these weapons would not be supported in service. During the same year, the first crews commenced training on the EHI Merlin HC3 helicopter at RAF Benson. This helicopter type was temporarily grounded, later in the year, following the loss of a Royal Navy variant off the coast of Scotland.

In August 2000, the aircrew categories of

navigator, air signaller and air electronics officer were merged into the single designation of Weapon Systems Operator. Following the grounding of the entire fleet of Tucano training aircraft in September 2000, some student pilots began training at Pearce Air Base, in Western Australia, in November of that year. The first of the new Lockheed Hercules C130J, with its reduced flight deck crew of two, became operational with No. 24 Squadron, at RAF Lyneham, at the end of 2000. The UK Government also committed the Royal Air Force to provide up to 72 aircraft as part of a new European Union Rapid Reaction Force

Early in March 2001, the first Merlin helicopter was delivered to No. 28 (Army Co-operation) Squadron at RAF Benson, while in May, the first Boeing C17 Globemaster III strategic transport aircraft formally entered RAF service with No. 99 Squadron at RAF Brize Norton. Later in 2001, the last permanently based RAF flying unit in Germany, No. 31 Squadron,

returned with their Tornados to RAF Marham, in Norfolk. This squadron was later designated as the lead squadron specialising with the Brimstone anti-tank weapon that became operational in 2005.

In the Middle East, the Royal Air Force continued to operate in conjunction with United States forces, in strikes against Iraqi air defence installations. The RAF also played a major role in a joint exercise in Oman, with troops from that country together with those from the UK's Joint Rapid Reaction Forces, in September and October 2001. This was the greatest test of the new rapid reaction force, and was the culmination of three years planning. The deployment involved over 24,000 UK personnel, and 55 aircraft from the RAF. This exercise came at a time when the RAF was already heavily committed in Afghanistan, following the events on September 11, with the provision of aircraft in support of the coalition anti-terrorist operations.

During the Fire Brigade Union's industrial dispute in 2002, over 3,000 Royal Air Force

personnel provided fire-fighting cover for the UK, in Operation Fresco. In that year, the Ministry of Defence announced the requirement for up to 150 Lockheed Martin F35 Joint Combat Aircraft (known as Joint Strike Fighter in US service) with a proposed in-service date of 2010, and the Advanced Short-Range Air-to-Air missile (ASRAAM) entered RAF service. However, there were further setbacks in the Nimrod MR4 upgrade program with the announcement of a reduction in the final number from 21 to 18 aircraft, together with a delayed service entry date of 2009.

The Bell Griffin HAR2 helicopter replaced the venerable Westland Wessex, when the Griffin entered Royal Air Force service with No. 84 Squadron, at RAF Akrotiri in Cyprus, in January 2003. This unit was led by the first woman to command a Royal Air Force flying unit, Squadron Leader Nicky Smith.

Afghanistan

Following the terrorist attacks on the United States on September 11 2001, since referred to as 9/11, Britain joined with the United States in military operations against the terrorist training camps of Al Qaeda, and the Taliban air defence targets in Afghanistan. These missions commenced, on October 7 2001, with bombing attacks by both United States and RAF aircraft. As well as carrying out attacks against terrorist targets, the civilian population was targeted in humanitarian operations

ABOVE
A400M transport aircraft is scheduled to replace the venerable Hercules C-130K in RAF service from 2009.

RIGHT
Members of No. 1 Squadron, Royal Air Force Regiment patrolling the perimeter of Basra air base in southern Iraq, October 2005.

involving an airlift of food and medical supplies. Following the initial operations, RAF aircraft played a major part in re-supply operations in support of ground forces, and also provided tankers for air-to-air refuelling of patrolling fighters and reconnaissance aircraft.

In late 2004, the Royal Air Force involvement in Afghanistan was increased, with the detachment of six Harrier GR7 aircraft of No. 1 Squadron, based in Kandahar. These aircraft, initially on a nine-month deployment, were placed under coalition control to provide close air-support and reconnaissance capability. The deployment was timed to assist in the maintenance of order during the presidential elections in October 2004. The detachment was later extended, in Operation Herrick, as British operations in Afghanistan are known, until August 2005. This date was, as often the case in previous deployments, somewhat optimistic, and the Harrier detachment was destined to continue for much longer than was first expected.

The main RAF base in Afghanistan is at Bagram, a station that has become the temporary home of many RAF personnel. The airfield is protected by squadrons of the RAF Regiment, and is the gateway for troops and equipment into the theatre of operations. RAF Hercules transport aircraft operate frequently from Bagram, as do the Chinook helicopters of No. 27 Squadron that have provided invaluable air transport for Royal Marines and Army personnel.

Iraqi Freedom

The air policing operations in the 'No-Fly' zones of Iraq were stood down in March 2003 in preparation for the commencement of Operation Telic, the British part of the US-led Operation Iraq Freedom. Operation Telic involved the movement of a vast amount of British troops, their equipment, and support services. The Royal Air Force commitment to the cause included almost one-third of its available strength in manpower, as well as large contributions to the strike, reconnaissance, and airborne refuelling requirements of the coalition forces. Many new types of equipment were used, in action, for the first time. These included the Raptor reconnaissance pod and the Alarm 2 anti-radiation missile for the Tornado GR4, and another new reconnaissance pod for the Harrier GR7. The Tornado also carried Storm Shadow, a long-range stand-off weapon, and the Enhanced Paveway precision strike weapon. The Harrier GR7 received the proven Raytheon Maverick precision all-weather strike weapon.

Chapter Ten

The initial assault on Iraq was decisive, with British ground troops gaining control of the Al Faw peninsula after being inserted into the area, and then supported, by the UK Joint Helicopter Command. The offensive operation was completed in a relatively short period. On May 1 2003, after a period of around five weeks, President Bush declared the end of major combat operations by coalition forces. Only one of the two main objectives of the action against Iraq was achieved, that being the removal from power of President Saddam Hussein, and his Ba'ath Party, from office. The former President of Iraq was finally captured on December 13 2003. The other major objective was to find, and nullify, the alleged 'weapons of mass destruction' that were believed by some to have been held by Iraq. These weapons have yet to be found.

Since the conflict, RAF assets have continued to be based in Iraq, thus maintaining an association with that country that has existed, almost continuously, since the formation of the service.

Future Strategic Tanker/Transport Aircraft

The UK Government policy of using outside agencies to provide equipment, buildings and services is likely to continue into the future, and covers a wide range of projects. Among these is the use of the Private Financial Initiative (PFI) in the replacement for the RAF tanker/transport fleet of VC10 in 2008, and the Lockheed Tristar, in 2012. As in most military procurements, these dates are provisional, and as such, subject to change. Under the PFI initiative, the RAF will pay for its in-flight refuelling, and some of its transport requirements, carried out under civilian contract arrangements over a 27-year period.

The contractor AirTanker Ltd will retain ownership of the aircraft, provide maintenance and training facilities, and may be required to supply some personnel. The contractor will also be able to use the aircraft for other commercial operations when not required by the RAF, the most likely scenarios being the provision of some in-flight refuelling, or possibly transport missions, for other European or NATO air forces. However, the RAF, as prime leaseholder, will have priority over any other user, and will be able to mobilise the entire fleet in times of crisis.

New Battlefield Eye in the Sky

The Raytheon Sentinel R1 is the designation for the RAF's ASTOR (Airborne Stand-Off Radar) aircraft. As a joint asset with the British Army, its role is to provide a platform from which

RIGHT First prototype of the Raytheon Sentinel R1 Airborne Stand-off Radar (ASTOR) aircraft.

BELOW Artist's impression of the Airbus A330-200 that will eventually replace the VC10 and Tristar in the strategic tanker and transport roles.

BELOW RIGHT Eurofighter Typhoon T1 two-seat trainer variant in No. 17 Squadron markings.

sometime in 2007. The first production Sentinel R1, which is based on the Bombardier BD-700 Global Express executive aircraft, made its 4.4 hour maiden flight on May 26 2004. It has a range of up to 6,500 miles, and endurance of up to 14 hours.

Digital Cockpit Training Aircraft

The planned procurement of the BAe Hawk Mk 128 Advanced Jet Trainer (AJT) features a fully digital cockpit, coupled with airborne simulation systems. This new version of the internationally successful Hawk will be used to train pilots to fly the new-generation, digital-cockpit fighter aircraft such as the Eurofighter Typhoon and the F-35 Joint Strike Fighter/Joint Combat Aircraft. The initial order for a batch of 20 aircraft, with an option for a further 24, is planned for a target entry into service from 2008. Pilots from both the Royal Air Force and Royal Navy will be trained on the new Hawk as part of the UK Military Flying Training System. In addition to its role as a training aircraft, the Hawk

battlefield and ground surveillance may be carried out, in a similar role to that of the American E-8 JSTARS aircraft. ASTOR was designed to be totally inter-operable with both JSTARS and the NATO Alliance Ground Surveillance (AGS) system.

No. 5 Squadron is the operator of the new Raytheon Sentinel R1 (ASTOR) aircraft and is based at RAF Waddington. Five aircraft have been ordered and all are expected to be fully operational

Mk128 will be capable of carrying out ground attack and air defence roles, in bad weather conditions, by day or night.

RAF Command Structure in 2006

As of June 2006, the RAF is currently organised into two commands: Strike Command, for the operational units, and Personnel & Training Command, for all training units. Tactical helicopter units are under the control of the multi-service Joint Helicopter Command.

Strike Command exerts overall command of its three constituent Groups. No. 1 Group is responsible for all air defence and strike attack/ offensive support aircraft, except for the Harrier.

No. 2 Group is responsible for front-line support aircraft such as transports, air refuelling tankers, and airborne early warning aircraft. No. 3 Group is responsible for maritime patrol aircraft, search and rescue helicopters, and Joint Force Harrier.

Personnel & Training Command is responsible for the flying training schools, university air squadrons and air cadet gliding schools. It also manages the service aspects of a number of training organisations operated by civilian contractors.

The trend towards the civilianisation of support services, which came to the fore in the latter decades of the 20th century, has continued into the first decade of the new millennium.

RIGHT
The Royal Air Force Falcons parachute display team making a spectacular descent. (© Crown Copyright)

BELOW
Lockheed Martin F-35 Joint Strike Fighter/Joint Combat Aircraft. Flags of the nine customer countries are displayed on the tail fin.

With the intention of maximising the effectiveness of the armed forces at the 'sharp end', the cost-effectiveness of the backup services has come under the scrutiny of those administering the contract tendering process. While there can be no doubt that some financial benefit may be gained by such means, there are those who have concerns regarding the future strength and capability of the service, faced as it is by several long-term commitments overseas, as well as the morale of its personnel.

According to MOD statistics published in April 2006, the *Trained* Strength of RAF personnel was almost 400 below the requirement of 47,290. The longer-term forecast is to achieve a manpower total of around 41,000 by April 2008. Assuming a reduced level of commitments overseas by that year, then this level of manpower can probably be justified. However, in the event of any additional call on RAF resources, or the continuance of ongoing deployments overseas, the planned reduction in personnel will come under even closer scrutiny. There is also the possible impact on service morale to be considered. The 2006 level of manning for trained full-time personnel in the Royal Air Force is less than a third of that in the 1980s: there is some cause for concern that this total is already much too low. The lessons to be learned from the past, particularly that of the 1939 period, should not be forgotten.

The Royal Air Force is justifiably proud of a history that spans a period of less than a hundred years. From the era of the balloon and kite, to the latest advances in technology, the RAF has evolved to face each new challenge. Whatever the future may hold there will be those who, '…Through Struggles to the Stars', will overcome adversity and add to its achievements, while upholding the values and traditions of their predecessors.

IMAGES SUPPLIED COURTESY OF:

GETTY IMAGES
101 Bayham Street, London NW10AG

EMPICS
www.empics.com

CODY IMAGES
www.codyimages.com

DEFENCE IMAGES
www.photos.mod.uk
© Crown Copyright/MOD,
Reproduced with the permission of the Controller of Her Majesty's Stationery Office

CONCEPT AND ART DIRECTION:
Vanessa and Kevin Gardner

DESIGN & ARTWORK:
Kevin Gardner

PROOFREADER:
Jane Pamenter

PUBLISHERS:
Vanessa Gardner & Jules Gammond

WRITTEN BY:
David Curnock

BIBLIOGRAPHY:

The Royal Air Force Today and Tomorrow: R.A.Mason – Ian Allan

The History of the RAF: Christopher Chant – Caxton Edition

INTERNET:
http://www.rafmuseum.org.uk/milestones-of-flight/timeline.html

www.raf.mod.uk/

www.bbc.co.uk/dna/ww2/